# SECRETS I'm D<sub></sub>

*Secrets I'm Dying to Tell You* explores author T
a suburb of Birmingham. The related essa
family, and some of his most intimate friends and acquaintances, many of whom were victims of abuse. Beginning with his mother's #MeToo stories, which were the impetus for this CNF collection, Barr began reconsidering the other stories he had heard or read about Bessemer's dark past—its embrace of the Ku Klux Klan, and its ongoing debilitating relation to Race. He also considered his own family background: the disloyalty he felt toward some family members because of their recklessness, their selfishness, their way of putting their own desires before the safety and well-being of those they should have been caring for. Finally, the secrets he ends with focus on the last part of his mother's life and how he tried to reconcile himself to loving and accepting her world, which he discovered was a world that he could still learn from, despite the belief that he was far more progressive than she ever was. Secrets can harm us, and though their revelation hurts, the only way we can heal is through such revelation and admission of our own part in the secret past.

"As I have noted before, Terry Barr is the absolute master of the familiar essay. I did not think it possible, but in this, his third collection, he travels further and deeper into his own and his hometown community's past. Barr is fearless, empathetic, and his relentless interrogation of memory and history results in discoveries that are both joyful and heartbreaking."—Tim Peeler Author of *West of Mercy* and *The Birdhouse*.

"In his new collection of essays, Terry Barr examines the ways in which privilege, memory, and pain embed themselves in our cities, our homes, our very bodies. The sense of humor that has earned Barr comparisons to Rick Bragg is still here, but filtered through a more serious lens. 'That was me, the quiet listener,' Barr writes, and as we read Secrets I'm Dying to Tell You, we're listening too, ears and hearts open as we reckon not only with the past, but with our responsibility to a shared future."—Joni Tevis, author of *The World Is On Fire*.

"'The past is never dead. It's not even past,' wrote William Faulkner, and that describes *Secrets I'm Dying to Tell You* by Terry Barr. Barr explores the world of Bessemer, Alabama, in a voice so real and true that it's like eavesdropping on a town's history with a trusted friend. Storyteller and archivist, Barr melds the past and present by asking the hard questions. Part love letter to his mother and part-mystery as he excavates the secrets of his hometown, Barr's voice is so rich and bone-real, you feel as though you were riding back in time on an Alabama summer night. Like Chip Brantley and Andrew Beck's podcast, "White Lies" we see the parallels of atoning for the ugly sins of the past by examining one's own connection to it through geography and family and what it means to be a son, a husband, and a father."—Kerry Madden, author of

More from writer Terry Barr

*Don't Date Baptists and Other Warnings From My Alabama Mother*

*We Might As Well Eat: How to Survive Tornadoes, Alabama Football, and Your Southern Family*

# SECRETS
# I'm Dying to
# Tell
# You

## Terry Barr

*5-16-21*

*For Kathy,*
*I hope you enjoy*
*reading these stories*
*+ all my secrets!*

*Warmly,*
*Terry*

**REDHAWK**
PUBLICATIONS

ISBN: 978-1-952485-09-1

Published by Redhawk Publications
          2550 US Hwy 70 SE
          Hickory NC 28602

Contact: Robert Canipe rcanipe@cvcc.edu

Contents:

# Introduction

*Dateline Bessemer, June 2020*

My friend Fred called me last week to ask if I had heard about the most recent murder in Bessemer. I wondered why this murder—sadly out of the too many occurring regularly in my hometown—should warrant a special call. But as Fred explained, this murder occurred right across the street from the house in which I was born and raised. I Googled the story on AL.com and saw a video of the murdered man's loved ones talking about the senselessness of the crime and its effect on them. I didn't know this family, but as I watched them standing on ground I knew intimately, I felt a certain pain and a more certain longing.

The place where I was raised is troubled, and I know so little and am so far removed from these troubles.

The house where this man's body was dumped is uninhabited, and for many hours, it kept a secret of something horrible that had been done there.

I called my brother Mike and told him. As we spoke, he did some Googling on his own, initially just to see the story. After a few minutes, and a very pregnant pause, he asked,

"Did you know that a Klan headquarters used to sit on Fourth Avenue in Bessemer, between 17th and 18th Street? This was back in the 1920's, but still."

I didn't know that.

But I wasn't surprised to learn it.

We all have secrets. Even and especially, towns have secrets— secret histories—which many don't know, and many more try to cover up or forget.

I don't keep secrets very well, as you'll discover in the essays following. Some secrets are lighter, even funny. Some are so well hidden— in basements, abandoned pieces of property, or just down the street from your seemingly safe house—that you'll likely never know them, or their potency on you and those you love, at all.

Actually, I can and do keep some secrets. So after reading these, imagine all that I haven't told—the stories that keep me awake on so many nights.

§

So much has happened since my last book was published. My mother and my mother-in-law both passed. Our beloved pet, Morgan, disappeared forever. The Bright Star's Jimmy Koikas also passed. And for the record, there's a pandemic, as well as marches and protests about the ongoing racial injustice in our nation. Like so many others, I often feel overwhelmed by life right now. And while my stories aren't specifically about our most current events, they do point to realities, histories, and, yes, secrets that have bearing on today. I hope you enjoy reading, and more than anything, I hope you are staying safe and wise, and that we all continue bending toward justice.

So, I dedicate this book to everyone I love—surely, you know who you are, even those of you who are gone.

"Listen...do you want to know a secret? Do you promise not to tell?"

—Terry Barr, June, 2020.

# Where Have We Been, Where Are We Going?

So my mother has a #MeToo story.

Too.

It began on a dark fall night in 1949, or maybe 1950. She was sixteen or seventeen and on a date. Of course it was a date, one with a boy she knew, a boy from the proverbial "nice family." I didn't know this story until recently, until the day Al Franken went bacterial. My mother will be 85 next week, and this is quite a story to hold for over seven decades. Her memory is sharp and long; the statute of lawful limitations, however, long gone.

I wonder: What is the statute of limitations for mothers telling their sons about their sexual errors, confusions, naiveté—the almost-perpetrated rapes of their past?

Twenty years ago my parents moved to a new neighborhood to escape the festering crime of their old one, which was on the hilly Southside of Bessemer where both my mother, and then I, grew up. In the vicinity of the house where she got married and where thirty years later I brought my own wife to visit, violence and drugs had grown so bad that a drive-by shooting on a summer Sunday afternoon finally pushed them to put their house on the market, to leave the community we had loved so dearly. I don't know all that happened before they moved, but since their move to their new and tonier neighborhood, my mother has been confiding in me, telling me stories of men, supposedly respectable and classy Bessemer citizens, who had made passes at her.

Many of these unwanted advances occurred while my dad was still alive.

The incident I heard in greatest detail concerned the neighbor who lived just up the hill in back of their new house. My mother had spoken to him across their mutual backyard numerous times. He seemed so cordial, so helpful, as they discussed their respective bordering shrubs, potential tree removal, upcoming neighborhood cookouts, and the best way to grill steaks and ribs.

"He went to Bessemer High School, too," my mother reported. "He was eight or nine years behind me, so of course I never knew him, but I had heard of his family. He was on the football team. His wife is a doctor in town, but I'm still not sure what he does. He seems to be always at home."

Apparently he had much free time; his wife worked long hours.

Like a good neighbor, this man gave my mother tips on workers to hire to remove the stumps and overgrown herbage in her yard. In turn, my mother hosted him and his wife and the other neighbors they knew for patio barbecues. These cookouts, mainly populated by people in their 60's and 70's, sounded delicious to me, what with the pork, the smoked sausage, the ribeyes, but I always winced when I thought of the artery-clogging, the cholesterol girths of my parents' crowd. Still, I was happy that my folks had settled so smoothly into their new place, that the community wasn't threatening, but safe.

Their new house was located in one of the most prominent, and of course still "white," sections of old Bessemer.

But there was always more to this neighborhood, more than met the eye.

Long before my parents moved there, I had heard tales about neighborhood couples' "key parties," and about the scions of wealthy neighborhood parents who had to be bailed out of jail, and sometimes arbitrated under courthouse tables after they wantonly and recklessly broke into downtown businesses, hurting or maybe even killing some guards.

We so easily forget the past, don't we, when forgetting serves our purpose.

Until a call comes in on a Sunday morning: my mother informing me about what happened the night before at one of their cookouts.

"Everything was fine at first," she said. "I knew that Bill [name changed] had had a few beers before he came over, I mean, I could smell that he had, but I didn't think much about it. I was too busy tending to the meat and had just gone back inside to get a platter to hold everything. That meat was ready to fall off the bone."

Ever the chef, she raved over texture, taste, and sauce for a while, because that is all, truly, that matters to her: pleasing her guests with delicious food.

My parents, truthfully, didn't drink. My father, never; my mother, maybe on that rare summer day when even she got too hot and thought a white wine spritzer just the thing to quench her thirst. She's from the era of genteel southern women who get worried and burdened if they truly have to go to the liquor store for cooking spirits. She's never forgotten being so intimidated when she went into the local state store to buy apricot brandy for a special pound cake. The clerk saw her nerves:

"Ok, but if I sell it to you, you have to promise me something."

"What?"

"When you finish baking that cake, you have to bring us some!"

That got a big laugh from the other clerks, but not so much from my mother, who took her package home and was so befuddled that she didn't start on the cake until the next morning.

Seeing any form of alcohol in our house also befuddled me, and when I finally brought home a six-pack of Michelob in my grad school days and put it in our refrigerator, I could hardly sleep that night. It all felt so wrong, so Snopesian.

As I reflected on these days of beer past, she continued her tale:

"So I was in the kitchen, and I heard the back door swing open. It was Bill. The next thing I knew, he was trying to pin me against the counter. 'Lemme kiss you,' he said. I pushed him off, and went back outside. He got so drunk then that his poor wife had to carry him back home. Your daddy helped put him in their car, but he never knew what that man tried to do, and I wouldn't tell him either."

Instead, she told me.

She was in her mid-sixties then. Her assaulter was my age now. I was in my early 40's when she told me, and living two states away. I remember putting the phone back on its station and finding my wife.

"A strange man tried to kiss my mother."

My wife looked at me.

"What did she do?"

"Pushed him off and went on serving supper, I think."

Maybe our daughters called to us then for a story or a snack. Maybe we talked about it later, but if we did, I don't remember. What I do remember is that I tried so hard to forget.

I don't know if this man ever apologized or tried to. I don't know if he claimed to not remember what he had done. I do know that he and his wife moved out of town a few months after this evening, as if "it" had never happened; as if they had never been there. No one ever complained.

Only the stories and heartaches remained.

∫

My father died in December, 2000. Within the next year, three different men asked my mother out. They were respectable men, and they behaved toward my mother respectably. She refused two of them, one being our family's apothecary, the other, a family friend who had lost his wife a few years before. The third became her steady companion for the following fifteen years, until he passed away in the summer of 2016. He and my mother had a comfortable kind of relationship. They lived just a few houses down from each other, but decided they didn't need to marry.

"I didn't want to have to wash another old man's dirty underwear," my mother explained.

One marriage seemed enough for her, though even when she was seeing her steady companion, another man, a church-going friend, tried to get close to her. She claimed not to care, but the one time I went with her to church, I saw her paying him attention. Still, when you're in your 80's, why not enjoy the attention, the company? We're all adults here, and *these* stories, at least, are funny, harmless. Good supper talk.

In quieter moments, say over winter vegetable soup and homemade cornbread, Mom might unravel some tales of her dating youth to my brother, my daughters, my wife, and me.

One boy she dated even gave her a ring, which she accepted.

"He was such a momma's boy though," she said, so while he was away at college, she started dating someone else.

"What happened to the ring, Granma?" my older daughter, Pari, asked.

"I wrote him a letter breaking it off, but he didn't write back, so I kept it," Mom said, laughing.

I don't know if my daughters respect her for this act, or are simply amused. I try not to think of this poor boy, expecting so much, and getting so rejected, especially while he was away trying to make a future for himself and my mother.

I guess many of our parents have such stories, such pasts. I guess I have a few myself. Nothing so abnormal, though perhaps some of my stories are a bit raw, maybe a bit mean, too.

Occasionally, and I have no clue as to its prompting, my mother will launch into a story from another place, a place I don't recognize as akin to her, as fitting *of* her. A divulged tale that beforehand I wouldn't have dreamed possible.

Throughout my childhood, my mother had a large circle of friends. One of these friends was a slightly older woman who shared my mother's passion for antiques and interior design. She could have been my mother's mentor, if my mother used such words.

This woman had a series of wire-haired terriers, each of whom was named "Wooly-Booger." I begged to go to this woman's house every time Mom went just so I could play with Wooly-Booger, who, despite the incarnation, was always rambunctious and loving. The house where we played, where Wooly-Booger lived, is on the same street where my mother now lives. A priest lives in the house now, and if that's not exactly strange, it's something.

When her friend lived there, though, she and her husband were prominent citizens in town; the husband, in fact, was some muckety-muck in Alabama politics. A real Wallace man, or so I was told. I don't recall it, but my mother told me I met him once. My image of him is fuzzy, nothing real or definite, just a short, white-haired overweight man, like so many others. They also owned a coastal house and invited my parents to spend random weekends there, which I'm sure was a treat given how frugal my father was.

It was on one of these weekends that my mother's friend's husband made a pass at my mother.

"He was drunk and disgusting," my mother said.

His wife found out and cried and apologized. Naturally, the friendship died.

"He was such a louse, and poor Estelle had such a time with him. But I couldn't stand to be around them anymore."

This couple suffered other tragedies, too, but despite it all, my mother kept my father from discovering what had happened that weekend. Dad was such a loner anyway, so another lost friendship didn't bother him. I might be missing some details of this story, but when I think about asking, I hesitate.

Don't I already know too much?

∫

Stories have a way of clotting in my mind. I've heard that you recognize the storyteller in your midst by the one who hardly ever speaks— the one you don't really notice, who sits quietly to the side, or just on the periphery of your vision. You imagine he or she is drawing, or listening to a transistor radio, or reading his new Batman comic book. You don't think your stories are seeping in, or ever will.

And you're so wrong.

That was me, the quiet listener, the one who had to stay close to the adults because their stories were far better, much more entertaining and valuable than the other kids' games going on around.

I would lurk in the backseat of our car, or at the other end of the kitchen table, or in the grass off our front porch. In these places I could hear the talk, the gossip, the scandals, communicated by adults enjoying after work hours, recounting what outraged them and, in turn, what mystified and stimulated me.

My Nanny, my mother's mother, lived with us. Actually, it was her house. I loved to listen to her talk, which she did frequently on the old black phone in our breakfast room. Coke bottle in hand, cigarette smoke filling the air, she told tales of brave Ulysses, or in this particular case, of a shiny, bald man at a pool party—a man who amused the party-goers by putting a woman's gold hoop clasped earring on his ear and pretending to be TV's Mr. Clean. He spoke with an accent (German, Hungarian?) and brought his teenager daughter to the party. He was a widower or a divorced parent. But at this party—one where everyone was encouraged to bring their kids—he did and was something else.

We had another family friend, a decorator for one of Birmingham's major department stores. She was a widow and in her 60s. She wore enormous hats and crazy wigs.

She also had an enormous bosom, and so Nanny's story picks up.

"That man kept sidling up to Imogene, just trying to get as close to her bosom as he could. And with his daughter there, too! Imogene just kept pushing him away, though!"

We went back to that party the following summer, and the same scene transpired, only this time with a man they called "Lefty."

I was nine and ten during these summers. Nanny never noticed or cared that I was listening to her stories. So what did I think? Mainly, I tried not to, but words and images, as I say, have a way of clotting. I kept seeing Miss Imogene pushing men off her bosom. I didn't exactly understand why they did it, but I didn't *not* understand it either.

I just didn't know that people I knew did such things, especially for others to see.

Another story I overheard concerned my father's mother, my MaMa. On the evening we buried her—she lived to be 99—my father played a tape recording she had made of the story of her life. She told about her marriage to George, my grandfather and namesake, whom I never knew. She told of her deep love for him. Still, she said, her marriage to him didn't stop other men from wanting to be near her, from coming round to their house at night (with or without my grandfather's knowledge, I don't know). Apparently, these men fell all over each other to dance with my grandmother:

"They loved my red hair [dyed], and they loved getting close to my bosom [real, or so I assume]."

My Dad and I were riding in the front seat of his car when she spoke these recorded words. What did he think or feel? He wouldn't say, though, just gave a random chuckle.

What did I think or feel? This was 1995. I had two daughters by then, the younger one, Layla, barely a year old. I couldn't speak, but just stared out the passenger window at the darkened landscape of North Birmingham as we drove home in the late October night.

What is there to say, after all, about your grandmother's ample bosom, and the men she indulged who wanted to get close to it?

§

Any of these could be #MeToo's, which makes me even sadder than usual. None of these, however, is the story I most want to tell.

We were driving home from the hospital on the Wednesday before Thanksgiving, my mother, brother, and I. Mom had a lung biopsy the day before, and fortunately, her cancer had not metastasized. Getting out of the UAB parking deck proved as long and as formidable as exiting an Alabama football game if you waited till the game clock hit 0:00. Her procedure took less time, it seemed.

So to combat rush hour interstate traffic, we decided to travel the old family route: down Second Avenue past old theaters like the Ritz, past the Sears building, and even past the tan brick building that formerly housed Standard Jewelry Company, where Dad worked for almost forty years. All are closed now, either boarded up or simply abandoned. This part of Birmingham might be beyond rehabilitation.

On this day we had already been exposed in the nuclear sense to revelations by an LA disc jockey that Al Franken had taken a picture of her on a plane as she slept, making it look like he was fondling her; that he had pressed his tongue into her mouth as they rehearsed a skit for overseas troops. We had seen the photos and coverage as we waited in the hospital for Mom's official release. I kept picturing Al's latest book lying on my shelf at home: *Al Franken, Giant of the Senate*. I was trying so hard not to fill in the blank (Giant _____?), and also trying so hard to decide what to do with my unfinished birthday gift. My friend Owen had presented me with the book the previous summer, just months before Owen succumbed to lung cancer himself—a surprise attack of aggressive, abnormal cells. I made it through Franken's *SNL* days, but never got to his Senate run and tenure. I just couldn't see picking it up again, but since it was a gift from my lost best friend, I couldn't part with it, either.

Mom, Mike (my brother), and I had grown sick of the Franken story, sickened by a lost liberal icon, who joined other fallen stars: Conyers, Weinstein, Spacey, Lauer.

Biopsy or not, my mom loves to focus on politics these days. You might describe her as a "Vomit-Trumper," meaning she feels like doing the former whenever she sees the latter. So as we drove home on Lomb Avenue, heading toward the Bessemer Super Highway, Mom began wondering how much of a chance Democratic Senate candidate Doug Jones had in his special election against Roy Moore, the alleged pedophile. She had already directed the entire nursing staff on her floor to vote for Jones:

"It's especially important that the Black folk turn out to vote," she urged, to every Black woman she came into contact with.

I have to admit to being embarrassed by her repeated statements, but this is Alabama, and a White woman urging Black women to get out and vote to defeat a White male sex offender has a certain "you-never-thought-you'd live-to-see-this" panache.

So as we discussed the election, each of us hoping for, but not so convinced of, a Jones victory, we passed Birmingham's Rickwood Field, the oldest continuously-used ballpark in America, and where I once saw Reggie Jackson play for the Birmingham A's. As I dreamed of Reggie, Mom told her nightmare.

"My God, all of this awful behavior! Well, it happened to me, too. I had agreed to go on a date with this boy. He took me to a dance at the Pickwick Club in 5 Points South, and we had a good time. Okay.

"After the dance was over, we got in his car, and I thought he was going to take me home. But he kept driving out of town, out onto roads I didn't know, a bad part of town. I kept asking him 'Where are we going?' but he wouldn't say anything. The next thing I knew, he had pulled onto a dirt road somewhere, stopped the car, and then he just lunged at me. I kept yelling at him to stop and take me home, and finally he did stop. But he wouldn't take me home.

"He drove back into Birmingham, and I was still scared, so I made him stop the car and let me out. We were on the eastern end of First Avenue, not a very good place, but I knew that if I could just get to the Tutwiler Hotel on 20th Street, I could get a cab, since there were always some waiting there. So he stopped the car, and I got out and walked."

She had to walk six city blocks after midnight in her ball gown and heels. All alone. When she reached the Tutwiler, she did find a cab, but she realized she had no money to pay him.

"I told him to please take me home and that my mother would give him the money when we got there. So he agreed, and when we got home, my mother blessed me out for leaving the house without any money! I knew better, too, but I was young, and you know how the young don't listen!"

I also know even more specifically what could have happened to my mother both in that car and after she escaped it.

In 1934, according to *Alabama Heritage* magazine, a Birmingham woman named Faye New was abducted and murdered not so far from where my mother walked. New's murder was never solved, or at least the alleged murderer was never convicted. Apparently, he, too, seemed like such a decent man beforehand, someone who supposedly was doing her a good turn http://www.alabamaheritage.com/from-the-vault/the-murder-of-faye-new.

As I listened to my mother's story, I wondered what her mother had or hadn't told her about boys and all that they might do under the circumstances. We think of teenage boys today as wild and reckless. But in the 1930's and 40's, they were just as much so. We just didn't have the sort of news cycles then as we have today.

"The next morning my mother called that boy's mother and blessed her out, too."

I think Mom's father was still alive at this point, but she didn't mention him. Maybe she kept it from him. But how? Maybe, like many men, he was asleep when she came in that night, trusting that, like usual, all was well. Maybe she wanted to forget his reaction, or lack of it. She has told me that he didn't suffer many fools, but that he was otherwise a gentle, kind man.

"So what happened when Nanny confronted the boy's mother?" I asked.

"Nothing. And I never saw him again."

She didn't tell us his name; this incident occurred during the years that her family had moved from Bessemer to Birmingham, so we likely wouldn't have known the family anyway. And even if we did, what would it matter? What would be gained?

Just the knowing.

§

We were getting to the outskirts of Bessemer now, where that old KKK "welcome" sign formerly stood. She told this story as if she were telling about a day at Pineview beach, west of Bessemer, as if it had happened only a week or so ago. She's a great storyteller, my mother, using the sort of vivid details that writers envy. As she talked, I saw it all, and I thought about how desperate she must have felt. How she must feel now. About how this evening must have scarred her; how fresh those scars seem to be. How often those scars were reopened over the years of her life.

No, this wasn't an actor who molested her, or a congressman, or the POTUS—no one with economic or political power over her. This was a high school boy, doing what so many have done and continue to do today, all across our country. They know better. I know they do.

And I know some who did even worse. They were from good families, too, ones we socialized and went to church with. They still are.

We keep these stories quiet, to ourselves, until the time and distance have grown so vast that no statute can re-open them, and even if it could, there would be too many who would disbelieve, or try to mitigate the circumstances, as they do within the statutes; as they tried to do to Roy Moore's accusers.

Perhaps even to Stormy Daniels.

We arrived home again, in the Alabama night, and my mother climbed the stairs to her house, the back stairs leading into the kitchen, a place of warmth and comfort, and a place where a man tried to press himself on her not that very long ago.

Why *does* my mother keep telling me these stories? Am I supposed to keep them to myself? Violate her trust, her privacy, by writing about them?

§

The weeks went by, my mother's biopsy incision refused to heal. In fact, it festered. "It hurts," she said, and I advised her to go to her doctor's the next day, which she did. Her doctor removed the stitches and prescribed treatment, but before that could work, my mother contracted pneumonia and was hospitalized again. It was two weeks before Christmas; she was supposed to be traveling up to our house for these holidays, and I doubted whether she'd be strong enough.

Or alive enough.

Her friends were looking after her and assured me that I didn't need to come down yet. When I called her room, she sounded okay enough. We even celebrated by phone Roy Moore's defeat—such a victory for Alabama, for victims of sexual predation. Mom's voice sounded clear, her spirit even willful. The day after, though, she sounded weaker:

"Something's wrong," she said. "I'm not getting any better."

"It takes time," I assured her. "You've been through a lot recently. Your body is tired, but please be patient."

What I didn't say was "Please don't give up yet." I don't know why I kept this to myself. Maybe was new territory and I didn't know how to cross it. Usually it was she who comforted me: "Don't worry, I'll get better someday."

Two days later I was at the hospital. Her doctor decided to release her, saying that she could recover just as easily, if not better, at home. On one level, I was relieved. On another, I was anxious about her precarious health and whether I could meet her needs.

I'd helped raise two children, though, and I was competent. I made us grilled cheese sandwiches and creamy tomato soup. I checked her blood pressure daily and encouraged her to take the medicine she hated. I tried not to ask too often if she was feeling better, because I didn't want to hear the opposite.

Days passed, and I heard her tell a friend that she was still planning to travel back to my house with me for Christmas. This encouraged me, and so I encouraged her. We made the trip, but a day after arriving, as I took her for last minute Christmas shopping and a late lunch, she said, "I don't know. I don't think I'm ever going to feel the same again."

My heart fluttered and sank.

On Christmas, day, however, after cooking the elaborate meal we'd come to expect of her, she declared that she was feeling better again, and indeed, she looked better, sounded better. She'd gotten through something once more, as, seemingly, she always has.

As she did twenty years ago after her neighbor tried to kiss her. As she did ten years before that when her friend's husband did something else.

And as she did nearly seventy years ago in a place she didn't know, with a boy she thought she could trust.

Though she recovered from these past assaults on her body, she stayed quiet about them for years, decades. I don't know that I've fully recognized before how strong her resolve is: to move on from trouble, to keep trouble to herself.

To stay quiet, to act as if what happened to her didn't really matter. As if her only choice, ever, was to keep going.

As if no one remembered what happened to her on those nights.

As if no one knew about these violations of her at all.

These thoughts make me pause. I am too naïve. Every woman has a #MeToo story. My wife, my daughters. So far and for some reason, they have spared me the telling. Are they, too, trying to stay quiet and strong? Do I want to know what I don't know, now?

So, I'm asking here:

Have your wounds ever fully healed? Must your scars be heard to *force* us to remember what we've done, where we've been? To *help* us remember to act more wisely in the future, wherever we are, wherever we're going?

# Daddy's Baby

Not so very long ago, on a *Facebook* page far far away, a casual acquaintance posted a query as to why we don't know anything about President Obama's past girlfriends. Why anyone would be so interested in such personal esoterica baffles me, though I suspect that if you believe the President isn't truly an American, you might also believe he's a body snatcher with invented history. I can just see the pod resting in some poor unsuspecting middle class half-Black person's garage. But knowing nothing about Obama's love history—though I like a scary invasion film as much as the next American—I decided to help the posters out by naming all of *my* past girlfriends. I had to rest after naming the first ten, and when I returned to Facebook, I was hit by posters who accused me of hijacking their thread—of being off-topic and impertinent. Someone might also have asked if I were a commie, which of course made the whole body-snatching metaphor even more perfect. I proceeded then to name the fifteen other girlfriends I hadn't gotten around to listing on the first try. This led to someone challenging me for an in person talk and coffee, but by then I had noticed something interesting about my own list.

The first six girls I dated were named either Kathy, Pam, or Patti.

I was sixteen on my first ever date, with Kathy. I was twenty-eight when I got married, and in those twelve years, there weren't but a few weeks when I wasn't dating someone. And yet, of the four or five recurring dreams I have—putting my car in reverse and not being able to stop before I crash into a brick wall being foremost—the scariest recurrence is that not only am I not married; I am completely bereft of marriageable prospects. My wife is always one of my dream-options, but somehow she remains elusive, or else I've chosen her but she's rejected me. Sometimes in the dream I know we're together, but it's like I can't believe it. Can't accept it or take it all in. I wake up from these dreams relieved and next to her, as I've been for the past thirty years.

I wonder to what degree my loneliness in these dreams stems from my early girlfriends rejecting me; some went out on me or told me not to call unless I had "something to say;" others were unwilling or unable to show physical love and desire. And I don't altogether mean sex.

At seventeen, I dated my first Pam for several months during the spring and summer. While we held hands often and she sat right next to me in the full-length front car seat, the only kiss I ever got from her was a chaste closed-mouth peck on my own anxious lips when we said goodnight. I liked Pam. I liked her family: her mom and her older brother and her Aunt Sadie. I don't remember what happened to Pam's dad, but I suspect he left them, or at least I don't recall any sadness when he was mentioned. Still, in my experience, a seventeen-year-old boy would like to be kissed more passionately if he could, and finally I broached that subject with Pam. Call me callous, but back then it didn't occur to me that Pam had never kissed anyone that way before. Or maybe I did realize this but just didn't care. After we talked, she agreed to "go parking" with me on our next date: Friday night's football game.

It was *her* high school's game, and after mixing with her friends both at the game and at Shakey's Pizza Parlor where they all hung out, I noticed that our parking time was diminishing, given her 11:00 curfew. We left Shakey's at 10:40, and I drove her home. I know I said something about being disappointed, and she nervously shrugged. When I walked her to her door, she turned, leaned in, and kissed me on the mouth, slipping just the barest trace of her tongue onto mine. The entire kiss lasted four seconds.

That was our last date, and think of me what you will, but remember that I was seventeen, and try to forgive me, as I've been trying for all those years to forgive myself.

My first Kathy was more experienced. For our first date, we went to see *Travels With My Aunt*. Neither of us appreciated Maggie Smith's performance or that this was Graham Greene's reminiscence of his boyhood. We were too busy holding onto each other. And when we kissed...

We went parking in my parents' Gran Torino on that first date, and on our second, she informed me that a) she was on the pill, and b) she didn't want to have sex. Moments later, she undid and pulled down both her and my pants. We did a lot, but I'm the type of guy who when told someone doesn't want to do something, promptly gives up. Kathy and I had other dates that always went this far, but we never had sex. After our sixth date, Kathy dumped me and went back to her old boyfriend, an older, long-haired guy with his own car. They seemed quite happy.

Kathy had an intact family, though her parents were at least twenty years older than mine. I thought a lot about her after she dumped me, and then one day I realized what she had said to me. And what she meant.

My other Kathy and Pam were shorter-lived experiences. Still, the coincidence of names is funny, and at some point, my parents asked me if I ever considered dating someone who was not named Pam or Kathy. As usual, I thought but never said that I was just happy to *be* dating. What did I care about names, ranks, serial numbers or religion? [Kathy was a Baptist and before I dated her, my mother warned me against straying into such forbidden territory.]

Next came my Patti's. My first Patti was someone I think I loved. There were moments when we connected like I dreamed a boy and girl should. Moments when she told me "I'm so glad to be with you again," for we had dated briefly once before. When we broke up the second time—after she stood me up for a date by leaving a note on her front door saying "Buddy, something's come up and I can't see you tonight"—I was devastated, not only because I thought I loved her, but because I didn't understand why she didn't want me.

Later I learned why. I learned what the boy who dated her right before we reconnected had done to her.

It took me a few months to get over her, and in some ways, maybe I never did. During those broken-up months I kept remembering the Christmas presents we exchanged: the silver bracelet I gave her, and the copy of James Taylor's *Walking Man* that she gave me. She told me how much she loved that album, particularly the song "Daddy's Baby" and what it meant to her. I had known all along that at some point in her childhood Patti's mother had walked out on her, her father, and her sister, though I didn't know the exact reasons or circumstances. I don't remember who told me about this, but certainly Patti never did. When we dated, she and her father lived in a green house on the slant of a slight hill. I wondered what it was like for the two of them living alone in that old house, and how empty it all seemed, especially at night.

"Daddy's baby, fussin and frettin,

What has you feeling so low?"

Was it something I'd never completely know?

It was only two years ago—a Facebook reconnection—when I discovered that the man she lived with was her stepfather, a man who married her mother, was left by that mother, but nevertheless raised Patti and her sister. It turns out that her mother didn't move out of town either, just far enough away to leave her family. Patti's leaving me made more sense then, for I was the least of her troubles.

Besides, James Taylor was never my favorite singer. I preferred Neil Young and David Bowie, and anything by the post-Beatles. In fact, it was a Paul McCartney song that led me to my second Patti.

∫

I'm at a dance at our rival high school on this Friday night. All my friends are gathered in the school gym, and local WERC-FM DJ Michael St. John is spinning tunes. St. John's Sunday night late show, "The Love Hour," is girl-famous. Every record he plays during the Hour carries a dedication. For instance, "The Way We Were," from Brenda to Donnie with love; or "Color My World to "that certain someone" from Darlene, with love; or "We May Never Pass This Way Again" with love, sent from the seniors to Mrs. Walker.

Being a renowned DJ amidst a pack of sixteen and seventeen-year old girls must be heady for St. John. He's dark and skinny with a semi-roguish mustache. About the only girl who doesn't hover near him is the new girl in school. The one who keeps walking past the circle of friends I'm standing with. She's looking for something: for some place to be, I think. And then Paul McCartney and Wings' "Jet" begins: "Da dat da da...."

And my friend Jane creeps closer to me:

"Why don't you go over there and ask her to dance? Her name's Patti, and you might just like her."

Though dancing isn't one of my strengths—and thinking back on it, I would have been stumped if I had been asked to name one of my strengths—I walk over to Patti and ask her to dance.

"Sure," she smiles.

I can't tell you here that we made a striking couple, dancing to a rock song whose beat was anything but regular. But whatever I was doing couldn't have been as strange as Patti's windmillish arm-propulsion. We keep at it, though, the words to "Jet" urging us on in our hopeful dance of romance.

When the song ends, we stand there as teenagers do, not knowing whether to chance another song; not knowing whether if we stop dancing there will be another song for us.

A few years later in a Southern Literature college course, I'll read for the first time William Faulkner's homage to the decaying South, *The Sound and the Fury,* and reach the scene where Caddy Compson explains to her brother Quentin why she took Dalton Ames as her lover. She says she looked at him one day and thought "might as well be him as another."

I hope I got that right. The point is that when I looked at Patti, it wasn't like I saw her as my future one and only, or even anything close to it. Yet even as I rewind the scene of her propelling arms and recall that while in that movement, she kept her eyes steady on mine, I hear myself asking her if she wants to go out with me sometime.

The music has changed, and St. John is off in a corner with some girl he could go to jail for. I leave the party then with my friend Jim, hoping that between one of us, we might have a whole joint.

"So did you ask that new girl out," he says as we drive the highlands of south Bessemer.

"Yeah, I did. Why do you ask?"

"I don't know. I guess she kind of bugs me."

It's a bold statement. Most guys will kid you about your dates or ask if you plan on "getting any" later on. Most guys won't offer judgment on their friend's opportunities, especially ones so young and fresh.

"Well, it's just a date," I say. "It's not like we're going to make this a regular thing."

The pot kicks in about then, and then the radio announces the opening riff of the original "Layla." We launch our air guitars and bleating vocals, and for the rest of the drive, Patti fades into the night but also into part of me.  The next day I call her and we plan our first date, doubling with Jane and her boyfriend Jimbo to the movies on the following Saturday night.

∫

Patti lived with her parents and brother in a newer part of town. Brick or stone ranch houses with pristine yards shaded by pine trees. There was a part of me that had always wanted to date a girl who lived in a comfortable brick home—one that communicated comfort, princess phones, upstairs bedrooms. Even today when I drive through certain neighborhoods on Saturday mornings, I feel envious of the sun gleaming through those trees and of the young boys who will be calling later that evening to pick up their girls.

Or maybe I'm just recalling Patti as she appeared at her front door that first night. As she asked the three of us inside to say Hi to her parents.

Patti's family went to our church, so I had seen them before but only from a distance. Her mother was what southerners call "a sweet woman." A bit meek but friendly enough. Her dad, though. Not what I expected, but then, my experience was limited to mainly absent or nearly comatose fathers, though once I did date a girl whose father was a police detective. I wonder if she ever got married.

Patti's dad was a white-haired but otherwise youthful-looking man, impeccably dressed with every white hair firmly in place. He strode up to me that night with a genuine smile, and hand stuck straight out:

"Buddy! How are you? Glad you're here!"

He looked me straight in the eye, too—a look I met for six or seven seconds before he moved on to greet Jane and Jimbo.

We all stood in Patti's living room for five or ten unsettling minutes as her dad asked us which movie we were seeing, about what time it would end, and if we wanted to return to their house afterward for more talk. He said that last part with more insistence than I ever imagined a father of one of my dates would employ.

"Sure," we all said, "that would be great."

He walked us outside then, and for a minute I had the strangest feeling that he was going to get in the car with us or even offer to drive.

"Be back by eleven," he called.

We hadn't told him that the movie we were taking his daughter to see was *The Other*, that eerie thriller about supposed twin brothers and their "grandmother." He thought we were seeing *American Graffiti*.

I had noticed before we got in the car that Patti was holding a shoe box. But it only speaks to the oddness of the evening that I didn't think to ask what was in the box or why she carried it until after we pulled away.

"It's popcorn," Patti said, and sure enough, she opened the lid and there was certainly popcorn for all tucked nicely into the container. "Dad thought why spend the money when we can bring our own?"

It's not like I had all the money in the world either. Still, walking into a theater with a shoe box full of popcorn didn't confer the coolness that sneaking beer into a drive-in did. Almost warm beer at a drive-in is fine. Cold salty shoe box popcorn in a theater? I suppose we ate it anyway, but my memory doesn't extend to those moments. Instead, it holds onto Patti sitting in the back seat with me, holding that shoe box. A Butler shoe box, I remember. She looked at me, half-smiling like she knew something else, something she wanted me to know too.

The film was as creepy as we hoped. For me, however, it didn't touch what else I felt, even though I couldn't have said then exactly what I did feel. What we all knew, though we didn't speak it aloud, was that no way were we going back into Patti's house when we returned. Jane said she had to get up early the next morning for church, and that did it. As I walked Patti to her door, I was wondering if we would kiss. I needn't have worried. We hadn't finished climbing the four porch steps when the front door opened.

"Did you guys have a good time? Come on in here!"

"Dad, Jane has to go home. There's church tomorrow, remember?"

"Oh yes. Well. Next time. Glad to see you Buddy!"

And he escorted his daughter inside. Patti turned quickly to smile and then the door closed.

At seventeen, you're liable to brave elements you'd never attempt at twenty-seven. I didn't know what to think other than families have their own habits and rules. How well did I like Patti? I don't know; there was something about her—that smile, or maybe I just couldn't let go so soon of a girl who brought popcorn to a movie. So we kept dating, and we made up times and events, altered times and places so we could be alone. Our place was the upper parking lot of the Kingdom Hall of Jehovah's Witnesses, the old Hall not far from Patti's house. We talked and kissed, and sometimes that kissing was passionate. But we didn't go far. I sensed that Patti wouldn't want to, though she never discouraged any move I made. Call me scared or naïve. I was certainly so with Kathy, but I prefer those labels to their opposite.

The only thing Patti insisted on was that she not miss her curfew. And so we were never late arriving back at her house, where we were always met at the door by her smiling father, every white hair on his head perfectly in place.

As I remember her, Patti had an ironic wit mixed with the right amount of naivety to keep both of us off balance. I'll never know if she felt unleveled at all, but together, we distorted each other's equilibrium. More than anything, when we spoke on the phone two or three nights a week, she continually questioned whether I really wanted to be going out with her. And if I did, why did I want to?

The truth is, I had no idea why I was dating her. High school boys seldom have reasons for their actions, or if they do, it usually amounts to wanting to have fun, to be more adult. To be both more and less responsible.

Sometimes, boys like me even want to fall in love.

But not with Patti.

We know that words can't do love justice. Or non-love. And we know that kids of this age simply grow tired of each other. They aren't ready for love, commitment, fidelity. Of course many never are.

How else can I say this: Patti and I just didn't have enough in common to last. That would have been too harsh to tell her, and maybe more telling about my character than hers. What I admitted to myself, though of course I never said anything of this to her, was that I didn't want her curfew, her rules.

Her father.

My own mother had once warned me: "When you get married, you marry her family too."

And then there were my friends. Even Jane and Jimbo thought Patti strange. Of course, Jim never wavered from his views. So you can say that I wanted to retain my close friends more than I wanted to figure out Patti and me. That's what I told myself anyway.

§

I believe that we choose to go to high school proms because we know that years later we'll want a record of how dashing we once were. And how foolish. Maybe I'm less nostalgic than the next person, but when I look at my senior prom portrait, I see a nut. For my tuxedo, I chose a pink jacket with a dovetail in back. Not content with that bit of dandyism, I accompanied the jacket with black trousers, black bow tie on ruffled dark pink shirt, a black top hat, and a cane.

My friend Jim, whom I was doubling with, dressed exactly the same. We consciously chose this outfit and we consciously chose to look alike, and if that doesn't scream that we were seventeen, I don't know what does.

When Jim came to pick me up that spring Saturday night, my mother took some photographs of the two of us, standing side by side in our front yard, resting on our delusional twin canes. It wasn't that she took these shots out of pride, either. Before I rented the tux she had instructed me to get a classy black number, one that would show me off as a budding GQ model. So her marking this occasion by shooting us in all our pomp and pink was her style of revenge. She still has those photos, too, right in the family album.

But my outfit was just the beginning stain of this night, the night of my senior prom. Next, was the fact that our prom was segregated. This was the spring of 1974, and even Bessemer schools had been integrated for nine years by then. Nothing says progress quite like choosing segregation, so "we" held our dance and the Black kids held theirs. Separate but equal, as far as anyone knew. I don't remember where the Black prom was held, but there was no way they topped our venue. I don't know who concocted our plan, who thought of and negotiated our site, but it was pure genius. In that seventeen year old way of genius, of course.

Our prom was held outside the city limits at the FOP Lodge of Green Springs. FOP. The Fraternal Order of...

Police.

Let's see. High school prom-goers staging their last formal night of "party" at a policeman's lodge. I feel I can't emphasize this enough. In Thomas Hardy's master poem "The Convergence of the Twain," he draws us into the unhappy but fated marriage of the Titanic and the Iceberg. On this prom night, the convergence was my friend Jim's flask of bourbon with one of the three policemen on duty. For Jim had barely gotten the flask open and begun pouring his spirits into his Coke, when the policeman appeared by his side, steered over as surely by that unseen hand as was Hardy's ship toward that block of ice.

"Good luck," the policeman said as he tipped the flask to his nose. "And Goodbye," as he put it in his pocket and escorted Jim and his date Melissa (who by the way I had to ask *for* Jim) out of the hall.

I knew at the time that this would be a precious memory. I also knew that I had just lost my ride home. Our ride, I should say, though Patti, at my side, didn't seem worried at all.

"Don't worry," I assured her. I'll ask Jimbo if we can hitch with them."

I asked him and Jimbo, of course, agreed, though I can still recall that look in his eyes—the look that says, "Well, you just fucked up my night."

Maybe that look was merely one of hating to share this night, both the rest of the dance, and the after-dance supper at Birmingham's Luau Restaurant, the top faux-Hawaiian rendezvous for high school revelers. Maybe he and Jane had plans beyond that supper even.

Or maybe his look was because he knew, like everyone else seemed to, that this was to be Patti's and my last date.

Maybe I didn't realize that everyone knew my intentions of breaking up with Patti after this night. As I think about it now, I'm sure I was much too preoccupied with looking good, with having a memorable night with my friends. And maybe with making Melissa, or Mary Jane, or Sheri—all of whom I had crushes on—see what they could have had.

Even as my eyes wandered on this night when I would dump Patti, I still could see that she looked gorgeous.

Stunning.

And this isn't the nostalgia of forty years talking. For I still have the portrait of us taken in front of the prom backdrop emblazoned with the theme song "Time In a Bottle," though in the picture, the "In" has somehow disappeared. Patti wore a floor-length silver-white gown, and she's holding the array of pink and white flowers I bought her. But it's her smile I remember mainly: genuine, hiding nothing, happy, at least as far as I can see.

But in that moment, standing behind her in my top hat and cane, I couldn't actually see her at all.

Jane had told me earlier that one of the changes that even I had noticed in Patti was her hair: "She rolled it. She wanted it to look especially good for tonight." Patti's hair was never full, never had much body, and usually hung in thinnish strings. But examine our photo carefully: her hair is lustrous, shining.

Memory gets a little foggy here. We must have stayed at the dance for three hours though I can't see how we filled that time. I do remember seeing one of my crushes, Sheri Sokol, enter with her date, Roger Chandler. I hadn't asked Sheri out because of the rumor that she'd date only Jewish guys, and I was just a half-member of that tribe. But there she was with Roger, and I know I stood there gaping and considering my lost opportunities.

But I did get to participate in my first and only "lead-out." Patti and I got in line with the other seniors and their dates, all awaiting our names to be called so that we could enter forever the timeless bottles of our high school legend. By this point in the year, Patti had been living in Bessemer for five months. She wasn't well-known, but she was known enough not to have *this* happen to her. The MC, a junior boy I had known well from my own neighborhood, made all the introductions, and when he got to us, it was "Buddy Barr and his date Patti Stratton."

Only, Patti's last name was Stanton.

That might be just a small thing, a blip on an otherwise momentous evening's enchanted radar.

Or it might have been the sign of our personal times.

Patti never said a word about the slight, and so we danced to Jim Croce's love anthem, and then to Seals and Croft's "We May Never Pass This Way Again," only proving that the DJ well understood his mission. But as S & C's plaintive cries reached their schmaltziest crescendo, something even stranger happened. Something true and memorable.

I leaned into Patti and kissed her right there in front of my friends, our police guards, and the entire arena of segregated JLHS attendees. And that kiss, passionate and at the moment meaningful, lasted a full minute by my internal calculations.

I don't know what got into me and I can't say why I did it. I didn't love Patti, and of course, as my bio at the end of this piece will tell you, I didn't marry her. Maybe I was swept away, overcome by romance or nostalgia. Maybe it was the slight of Patti's name. Or maybe, I simply wanted one intimate moment in the senior prom I had dreamed of.

Later that night when I walked Patti to her door, another, even more impossible thing happened: her dad was nowhere to be found. Which gave us the opportunity to say all we needed about this night. About us:

"Thank you for not backing out tonight," Patti said.

"Oh, what are you talking about?"

"I know. But thank you anyway Buddy."

And that was it.

I had heard from Jane that Patti was going to ask me to her high school's prom, and if she had, I would have gone. That, I had thought, would be our true last date. But she never asked, proving at least that Patti understood me more than I ever did her.

She asked another guy, and Jane, who went to the dance, reported that during some love song, perhaps McCartney's "My Love," Patti and her date stopped the crowd by kissing longingly on the dance floor. It was strange to hear, but not the strangest thing I would hear.

After these events, I'd see Patti at church some, but soon I was off to college, and Patti, like so many others in our lives, passed into another way.

But in the odd and sad way that the details and clues of life manage to find us no matter what, I heard a story about Patti when I was home from college one weekend. My mother and Patti's had become Garden Club friends after Patti's mother divorced her dad.

"Apparently," my mother said, "Patti's dad used to beat Patti and her mother and brother too. Bad."

I didn't ask and my mother didn't speak about any sexual abuse. This was in the late 1970's though, and we weren't as frank and open as we are now.

But I keep picturing Patti on that last night at her door. I keep hearing her words, "Thanks for not backing out." I didn't understand then what was behind those words, that smile, her steady but questioning eyes.

Or behind her closed front door when she opened it that night, or any other night, and walked on through.

# Loyalty Oath

"Your mother is afraid you're becoming a gambler just like your grandmother," my son-in-law, Taylor, says as we stand over the craps table.

Taylor is twenty-nine. I am sixty-one. My mother is eighty-five.

I swear, I am not becoming like my grandmother. And even if I were to model myself after or merge my identity with someone else, my grandmother would rate on that list somewhere between Ayn Rand and Roy Cohn, both of whom, like my grandmother, were nominally Jewish.

The grandmother in question, my paternal grandmother Inez, has been dead for twenty-two years. My mother's fear of her power, however, seems to be alive and well. I can understand her fear and worry, I believe, for I know the story behind it.

Although the more I dig, the more I discover that I don't know that story as well as I thought.

§

**Ante Up.**

My hometown of Bessemer (a suburb of Birmingham) used to be a hotbed of corruption (both criminal and police), a wide-open town through at least the 1980's when I finally left, thereby missing the Bessemer courthouse bombing, another story for another audience.

In his recent account of one of Bessemer law enforcement's more heinous deeds, *He Calls Me By Lightning*, Samford University historian Jonathan Bass says this about Bessemer's sordid past:

> More than eighteen saloons operated in the Bessemer business district during these years (1887-1920), and most of them were infested with the rotten sins of gambling and prostitution. Lawbreaking stalked at the doorways of such evil...Gatherings of whiskey drinkers, fallen women, and cardsharps led to frequent bloodlettings. To minimize the violence occurring inside the ornate saloons, burly bartenders

forced the ruckus out onto Bessemer's streets, where ruffians brawled, punched, kicked, gouged, bit, sliced, stabbed, shot, and died in a slew of slag, mud, blood, and whiskey...dog, bear, cock, and wildcat fights [were] held in pits near the center of town, where [miners] placed bets with their hard-earned wages.

Professional gamblers set up shop in this frontier atmosphere and profited mightily from games of blackjack, craps, and five-card stud. Each day, trains arrived from Birmingham and other areas of the South with 'gambling dandies' aboard; travelers hoped to participate in the city's free-flowing 'sporting activities' and the 'unusual array of corruption and wickedness.'

All this activity thrived in spite of city ordinances outlawing gambling houses, cockfighting, and all games and sports of an 'indecent character' (Bass 21-2).


Bessemer, where my maternal grandparents lived and worked, where my mother was raised. Where I was born.

Marked.

I used to feel nostalgic about Bessemer. But nostalgia is an attempt to view again with a child's eyes. I saw much as a child, but not as much as there was to see of the avenues of vice in my home area.

My grandmother Inez, whom I called MaMa, was born in 1896, in Birmingham. Of the many memories I have of MaMa is the one when she taught me how to shoot craps. I must have been seven or eight. We used my Monopoly dice, and MaMa taught me that sevens were good on the first throw and elevens, anytime. I didn't ask how or where she learned to throw dice, and where she played when she wasn't with me. It was a game, and I saw nothing wrong with it especially when she said she won a lot of nickels playing.

A nickel was halfway to a comic book, and a full package of baseball cards back in 1962.

I have since learned where she played, but before I get to that story, I need to say that MaMa was a woman who freely and frequently told me about her boyfriends; who, in her 60's, when out to nightclubs on weekends; who kept an ongoing subscription to *Cosmopolitan* magazine; who thought UNICEF was a communist plot.

Who once defended Joe McCarthy to me when I was in grad school and learning about the "naming names" golden era of embarrassing American history.

"I loved Joe McCarthy," she told me. "He was a handsome man, and he knew all about those communists, too. He was right about them!"

I wonder if she ever knew or merely discounted all the loyal Americans, and especially the American Jews, McCarthy defamed and destroyed? But I never asked her. I suppose I was being loyal to Dad, but maybe, too, I didn't want to hear whatever response she would make. One can take only so much pain and disloyalty, after all.

Yet, this woman who thought communists were everywhere also thought aliens lived inside the earth and peeked out from time to time. Maybe it was the fear of such sightings—communists, aliens—that caused her to refuse to leave her apartment after she turned seventy, even to attend her own daughter's funeral. She still held card games at her place, and maybe she won enough grocery money to satisfy herself, though I know from later experience that playing against her was frustrating.

In games of Pinochle, where nines are the lowest-ranked card and there are two of every card, MaMa would call "misdeal" if she were dealt more than four nines on any hand. This is not a Pinochle rule. Naturally, as my mother lamented,

"If MaMa had five nines, that meant the rest of us likely had a very good hand. But she'd throw her cards in, and we'd have to throw ours in, too. Sometimes, I could have screamed! But your daddy would just laugh as if what she did was the funniest and most endearing thing ever!"

Though she was a force, MaMa also declared early in her life that,

"The one place I won't ever live is Bessemer. It's too wide open!"

Maybe that's why my father also declared, during the years when the bus he rode every week from Birmingham to the University of Alabama in Tuscaloosa made its regular stop in the Marvel City, that Bessemer was "one town I'll never live in."

Of course, after he married my mother, Dad lived in Bessemer from 1952 until his death in 2000. Forty-eight years. He visited the town often as a boy since his own paternal grandparents lived there. Was he against Bessemer originally because his mother biased him against it? Did something bad happen to him there? Was it "too wide open" for him, too, even in the late 1940's?

He never gave me his reasons, yet he always seemed glad to get back home to Bessemer from work or from any of our weekly trips to MaMa's. Still, it was Birmingham that he claimed to love; Bessemer was merely the place he came home to, a place MaMa only rarely visited even after her two grandsons were born.

It strikes me as odd that MaMa was intimidated by Bessemer's vice. Maybe she had a run-in with a saloon-keeper there. Maybe she lost a lot of money in one of the city's gambling dens. Maybe there was a man there who wanted her, chased her.

That I consider any of these alternatives viable should tell a reader all he or she needs to know.

Except there's more.

There's Little Man Popwell's place, where MaMa was a regular.

∫

**Dice Up.**

When Ma Ma showed me how to roll dice and explained the vagaries of this innocently illegal game (she never admitted its illegality, or claimed its innocence for that matter), I understood one thing: I couldn't always count on the "seven" to be loyal to me. Not that I used the word "loyal" then. Only now do I understand what seven promises. And only now do I understand that those standing at a craps table are not all betting *with* the roller. "Gambling loyalty" is truly a canonized oxymoron.

But what of family loyalty?

I know that I was not the only kid caught in the trap of jealous and suspicious familial behavior, of in-laws not trusting or being loyal to each other, of certain elders courting my allegiance to them by offering me bribes to stay at home with them or to call them often. We each have to negotiate for ourselves a way out of that trap, if we ever do get out. I was fortunate that when I got married and had children of my own, I was also willing to undergo therapy. There, I discovered the term "triangulation" as it applies to family: a mother, her husband, and his mother, for instance.

The triangulation that strangled my adolescence.

The sense of loyalty that was instilled in me; that I was staked to without understanding its odds, the nature of the bet.

My father, according to my mother, worshipped MaMa while my mother, according to my mother, felt belittled by her:

"When we first got married, I tried and tried to please her, to get her to accept me, to show your daddy that I was as good as she was, but nothing I did was ever good enough, never as good as what she did, or was. When I'd send her fresh cooked summer vegetables, your daddy would bring them home again because she'd only eat frozen vegetables. She thought the fresh ones were full of poison. And after I had gone to all the trouble of shelling peas and scraping corn just for her! And your daddy wouldn't say anything to her, wouldn't take my part ever."

When betting at a craps table, you learn quickly that sevens can be good to you on one roll but utterly destructive on another--not unlike quaint family gatherings every Sunday evening at Ma Ma's place. What seems good and right on one Sunday, can turn mean and nasty—and perhaps worse, *silent*—on another.

The luck of the dice. Or of who had control of them.

On the lucky sevens of our every-Sunday-at-MaMa's experience, we'd grill burgers, play games of Bingo or Parcheesi, watch "Lassie" and "Dennis the Menace," and have ice cream sundaes. On the ride home, maybe a detour through glittering downtown Birmingham, a stop at Kiddie

Land in Fair Park, or at the local drugstore for another pack of football cards or a comic book.

On the "craps" Sundays: a ride home in the car, dark shadows enveloping my brother and me in the back seat. A "discussion" over whether or not we could play football in our own front yard, mother for, but father against, because we'd,

> "...trample the grass. I work too hard to watch my grass get destroyed!"

Which then led to,

> "Well if you feel that way, then why don't you just go live with your mother! That's where it seems like you're the happiest." I was nine or ten on this Sunday night, and as my mother slunk against the passenger door and my father got frighteningly quiet, I was certain they would divorce.

They didn't, but the trips to MaMa's every Sunday continued, because the only way to win is to keep playing.

Or so I thought.

MaMa taught me to roll dice on a day I spent alone with her, a day over summer vacation. Using those hard plastic red dice, she rolled and rolled and let me roll, too. It was fun, and we used pennies, and whether I won or lost, she let me keep all the pennies in the end. She, or my Aunt Carole, would take me to the village Rexall afterward so I could use my pennies to buy a comic book. Always Batman, the law and order vigilante.

Maybe it was this same day. The games were put away, and I was sitting on MaMa's plastic-covered sofa waiting for Dad to come get me.

"Where is your daddy?" MaMa was beginning to boil. "He's late. He better get here soon because I have to go. I have a date!"

My dad arrived soon after, but MaMa was still angry. She barely acknowledged him and ushered us out of her apartment. Though I was young, the message to me was clear: MaMa had a boyfriend just like our babysitter, Mary Margaret, the fourteen year-old girl who lived down the street from us, did.

The other clarity: I was not welcome when MaMa's boyfriend arrived.

Occasionally, MaMa would show me pictures of the men she called her "boyfriends." These, though, were glossy headshots of talk show DJs across America. There was one in Boston, in Philadelphia, in New York, and Chicago. They all signed their photos, dedicated not to the one they loved, but just to "Inez, with great affection."

Recently, Mom told me more about one of MaMa's real boyfriends, maybe the one who came over that day after Dad and I left:

"His name was Jack Mendelsohn," she said. "And once, she showed your daddy and me a gift he got her: a silky negligee and matching robe."

I assume she "modeled" her gift for Jack. MaMa had to have been seventy at this point, yet she still focused on what was sexy, what was seductive. And make no mistake: she *was* seductive. I wonder now what my daddy thought when his mother showed him the negligee that her boyfriend gave her? What must he have felt? How did this sight affect his love for her, his loyalty to her?

Yet I know he had a way of misreading her, of not seeing or hearing what she did or said. I experienced it firsthand.

On the cassette tape where she recorded her life story, and which Dad and I heard for the first time on the way home from her funeral, she described the house parties she used to have in the 1920's and 30's, complete with games, music, and dancing. On the tape, she doesn't say if my grandfather was at home, at work, or if he was there:

"Oh, we'd all dance, and the men loved dancing with me. They loved my flaming red hair and getting up next to my bosoms."

Dead or not, one's grandmother's bosoms are potent things.

My dad, who only chuckled during our listening, played the tape later for my mother, who, out of Dad's hearing, remarked,

"I'm not surprised, and I'll tell you another thing. One night we were at her apartment playing bridge, and your daddy did something to make her mad. They were partners—they were always partners—and maybe he overtrumped her or maybe she just didn't hear his bid. Anyway, the next thing I know, she called him a 'liar,' and told us all that he had been a liar ever since he was a little boy when he said he woke up one night and saw a strange man standing in the hallway wearing nothing but his underwear."

My mother paused a moment, "I know one thing, your daddy might have worshipped her, but he was not a liar!"

"She was having an affair?"

"That's what I think."

It's a funny thing, your, *my*, grandmother's life. I never knew my grandfather, so MaMa was an island for me. Alone. Why shouldn't she date? And what if she *was* having an affair back then? Why should I care?

I saw her every Sunday afternoon from infancy until I was eighteen; on Thanksgiving and Christmas days; on those days I spent alone with her in summertime. I thought mainly that she was fun. What did I know of her world, her desires? Or even what her marriage was like?

I do know that her troubles with her triangular marriage still bother my mother now, twenty-two years after MaMa died. I know that it still disturbs the history of what she had hoped would be a loving marriage to my dad, even though he's been dead for seventeen years. Maybe the better question is why does it still bother me? Everyone else who is part of this story has crapped out by now.

What I do know is that from the time I started college, my mother started confiding her hatred for MaMa to me, though I had felt uneasy about it, sensed her ill feelings in the years before. When she confessed that hatred, I felt divided, split. I didn't hate MaMa, but felt horribly disloyal to my mother if I ever spoke well of or did something nice for my grandmother. I didn't know how to describe that feeling then; now I'll say it felt like doing something illegal, something like crossing the county line to go to some gangster's den. Something done without permission; something that I would never get permission to do if I was ever bold enough to ask for it.

Or something like examining MaMa's *Cosmopolitan* one late August day and finding Raquel Welch in her own skimpy lingerie, a still from *Bedazzled*. MaMa snatched that Cosmo out of my hands and stuck a copy of *The Plain Truth*, some sort of Biblical digest, in them instead.

"You can't be looking at that, Buddy," she said, even though it was out there in plain sight, within my grasp. I lusted after Raquel Welch for years, but from that scene on and even now, I can't envision that 60's sex bomb without also seeing my grandmother who, of course, also loved her lingerie.

Now that's quite a lesson, triangulation. I'd give it a "four" on the craps table: a three and a one.

§

### Six the Hard Way

"Buddy, I was so worried that you were going to lose all your money at that dice table. It's just how MaMa lost all her grocery money."

My mother has become a habitual worrier. She dates this change in her attitude back to the summer of her hysterectomy, 1971. She used to be more carefree, she says, and in my memory of her before the operation, that seems right.

After all, long ago she once spent a Saturday night in a gambling den.

Here, now, at The Greenbrier, the posh resort in the West Virginia mountains, though she's been playing the penny slots, she worries about me at the craps table where my son-in-law Taylor is showing me how to roll properly, and accurately detailing what the rolls and bets mean.

You have to be a guest at The Greenbrier to play. There are no bridges here leading to the entrance, no steel cages or peepholes to keep out unwanted players. A mere $400 a night per room will get you in.

I started the night betting with $60, and now I've doubled it. When my mother walks up and tells me she lost her money fast, though she had gotten up to $60 herself, she hovers a minute longer.

"This just scares me."

I wonder: does she know me at all? Does she think I'm a speculator? A habitual gambler? A man free and easy with his money?

In no other way do I remotely resemble my grandmother.

Unlike that woman, I am a natural red head, though my color has dulled considerably. And most unlike her, I am neither selfish nor unnaturally self-absorbed.

As my mother's words resound, Taylor looks me over, but he isn't thinking about any similarity between members of my family. It's simply my turn to roll again.

My daughters escort my mother to her room, finally. I could cash in and put her at ease for the time being. But I'm having fun at this table with my son-in-law. When I decide to stop, I am up $350. Taylor tells me I've quit too soon, because the next roller is a virgin to the game. Indeed, she rolls four or five seven's in a row, and squeals louder each time that precious and fickle number comes up. If I had stayed, I would have won $40 or $50 more. But I'm content. I wish Taylor had been, but that's craps for you.

The next morning, I report my winnings to my mother. She's glad for me, but I don't think she's any less troubled by what she saw the previous night. Indeed, old risks die hard.

§

## Holding Your Bet

My parents married in October 1952. I was born in July 1956. I am their oldest child. I was raised in the house where they were married, the house my mother grew up in. As if my parents' residential backgrounds weren't already different, there is this other factor: my mother is Protestant, my father, Jewish. This difference explains why they married in my mother's house. Before the marriage, they agreed that their children would be raised in my mother's Methodist church, but that they would ask my father's Birmingham rabbi to perform their ceremony. Dad's rabbi balked, however, at the children-being-raised-Christian agreement. It took them a while to find a rabbi to officiate. Bessemer's rabbi refused, too, so finally, a Montgomery rabbi, Rabbi Blachschlegel, agreed.

MaMa resented something about all of this, though specifically what is anyone's guess. She was not a faithful temple attendee; for God's sake, she used to accompany my Aunt Carole to nightclubs like The Boom Boom Room on Friday and Saturday nights. My mother believes MaMa viewed their marriage as just another way Dad might escape her clutches—that being married, he would no longer be so readily under her thumb.

That his loyalty to her would be divided or would reside somewhere away from her.

That he might have reason to tell about things he experienced growing up. Things he saw.

Strangers in his house.

My mother was scarred by the first years of her marriage, so she is prone to seeing triangulated binaries when they aren't really there. When she learned that I had gotten married in secret, her first words to me were:

"Well, your hers now," as if my loyalty had to be as divided as my father's was.

Still, her scarring is real.

MaMa refused to go to any of my parents' engagement parties or my mother's bridal showers. She did go to the wedding. I've seen the photos, one of which used to sit on her bedside table. There she is, holding on to my grandfather, George, and standing to the side of my wedded parents. Next to her are my dad's sister Carole and his brother Shirleigh. Everyone is smiling, almost as if they all got along and truly liked each other.

Almost as if they thought this photograph would be all anyone would know of them, or remember.

My mother has an album of wedding photos, but this portrait of my father's family on supposedly the happiest day of his life is not included in her book. I don't know what happened to that picture after MaMa died. I think I'd like to have it, though I wonder what I would do with it? It would feel strange to place it in my house, and also strange not to, this this portrait of a family as happy people, this captured memory from my parents' wedding night, October 1952.

§

**The House Rules.**

I have other photographs, though.

Go forward six months to the spring of 1953, a Saturday morning in May.

"Mother wants us to take her to Little Man Popwell's tonight," my dad says to Mom.

That my mother agreed to go amazes me. That her mother, my Nanny, didn't succeed in stopping them, amazes me more. Until that day, neither of my parents had ever been gambling. They didn't drink, but they weren't prudes because they went to New Orleans for their honeymoon. Or maybe that was just an Old South thing to do.

My mother tells this story of the first time she ever set foot in a liquor store, the state-controlled liquor store on Bessemer's First Avenue. It was 1966, and she had been given a new pound cake recipe, one that called for Apricot brandy.

"If my daddy were alive and knew I had gone into that liquor store, he would have died or killed me!"

But she survived, and the pound cake was incredible.

She wouldn't go into The Stadium Grill, either, even though it was just a hamburger joint that also sold beer across the street from Bessemer Stadium (Home of Champions), because Nanny told her that a man had once been shot there. Nanny also refused to go to Cliff's Barbecue just a block away from the stadium because she claimed that the owner and chef, Cliff himself, once had TB. Nevertheless, my mother took my brother Mike and me to Cliff's often. I loved the cheeseburgers and the jukebox, which had scrolling window units at every booth. To my knowledge, nothing there ever made me sick, except when I realized that the back window existed only to serve the Black clientele who could not, of course, dine in.

So my mother was what you'd call careful, though not completely temperate. Her idea of a night out consisted of finer things: supper at Bessemer's Bright Star or Birmingham's Joy Young, a show at the Alabama or Ritz, dancing at The Club high atop Red Mountain. On many occasions I watched her get dressed to the nines, my glamorous mother, and my dad escorting her, dressed in a dark suit and black wing-tips. Dad loved the movies, though expensive dinners gave him the heebie-jeebies. He tried to please his wife, to take her to the best places, but like my mother, he passed on anything seedy or dangerous.

None of this mattered, however, when it came to MaMa, who, outside of Bessemer, never met a place that wasn't too wide open, thrilling, seedy, or prone to being raided.

Dad was incredibly loyal to his mother. He once argued with me that the name of the Tex-Mex country singer was Freddy *Bender*, not *Fender*, because MaMa told him so. I don't know that I ever convinced him otherwise. He was equally loyal to his job, working for Ma Ma's brother-in-law, Mose, and his son, Arnold. Dad worked for over thirty-five years at their business. By the end of his twenty-sixth year, he was making $28,000. My mother says that after they got married, Dad got a fifty-cent per week raise, and given his yearly salary in 1977, I'd say that adds up right.

There is just something about family: often the better you treat them, the harder and swifter they crap on you.

So on this Saturday night in early May 1953, Dad chose loyalty to his mother over safety. He drove the three of them deep into the rural woodlands of Shelby County.

To go gambling.

Illegally.

At "Little Man Popwell's."

The very name conjures gambling, corruption, speakeasies.

The Mob.

I ask Mom now if she remembers now how to get to Little Man Popwell's.

"I have no idea, but I can tell you that it was way out in the woods, and you had to cross some kind of bridge to get to his house. You knocked on the door, and they could see you through the peephole, and if they knew you, they'd open the door. And they let us in immediately."

MaMa, it seems, was a known quantity.

My mother's memory is true.

I verified it when I obtained a photo from EBay, taken in 1951, showing four Birmingham policemen raiding Little Man Popwell's casino. In clear focus is the steel gate they had to walk through, enclosing them from all sides and from above. The front door has a grilled window and another door behind it where, presumably, the peephole rests. A bare light bulb hangs above, and the policemen are wearing raincoats and felt hats. Though they are out of their jurisdiction (Birmingham is in Jefferson County, not Shelby where this raid took place), apparently they had a search warrant issued by Shelby County authorities. Also from what I have learned, such raids of Popwell's premises occurred regularly.

Once inside, Mom remembers that the three of them went down into the basement where all the gambling tables—craps, blackjack, poker, and roulette—were set up and running.

"You daddy and I just stood there watching MaMa go from table to table. It seemed like we were there for hours. All we did was follow her around. We never played. She tossed the dice like she had done it a million times. Finally, she lost all her money and we could leave. I was so tired that night after we got home, and so was your daddy. He said he'd never do that again, and we didn't."

They definitely didn't, for exactly a week later, as they were leaving the Alabama Theater after a showing of some beautiful movie, the paper boys hit the Birmingham streets, hawking an extra edition of *The Birmingham News,* proclaiming that Little Man Popwell's club had been raided, and Little Man himself, arrested.

"What if it had happened a week earlier when we were there?" my mother asks now.

What indeed? My parents, raided, arrested, criminally liable for their associations.

My mother doesn't remember the date of the raid, but I have it. It's easy these days to find random facts, incriminating stories about your own familial past. Short routes to a place you might call home, or somebody's home anyway.

Somebody like Julius Oral "Little Man" Popwell.

§

## Cashing Out

The major raid at Little Man's, the one that fate spared my family from experiencing by exactly one week, occurred on Saturday night, May 9, 1953, according to a story by Bill Mobley in the April 3rd, 1954, edition of *The Birmingham Post-Herald*. The raid occurred at ...

> Popwell's Shelby County retreat just off the Florida
> ShortRoute...The fortress-like Popwell living quarters were
> raided by Birmingham police...an acetylene torch was used...
> to burn through a steel wire cage protruding from the front
> door. A hole was also burned through the steel front door when
> Little Man tried to argue the legality of the raid ("'Little Man'
> Sentenced to Year, Day: Guilty Plea Made Without Trial," BPH,
> Saturday April 3, 1954, 1-2).

Apparently, between forty and fifty "guests" were arrested that night and ordered to pay $50 plus court costs when they appeared before a judge in nearby Columbiana, which is Shelby County's seat. Popwell himself was sentenced to a year and a day in prison and made to pay $250 in fines plus court costs. He pled guilty to "displaying gambling equipment" ("'Little Man' Sentenced...").

The stuff of legends, and there's more: according to a story in *The Poker News*, despite his arrest, Popwell continued playing various forms of poker until his death of cancer in 1966 ("From the Poker Vaults: The Pride of Alabama," www.pokernews.com). This source also declares that stories about Popwell's generosity were legendary. Described by many as "honorable," Popwell once allowed a Birmingham toy manufacturer to pay off his enormous gambling debts "...in toys, which Popwell then distributed to the poor children living in the hills just outside of Birmingham." Many considered him a "soft touch," and "local bank officers" would often travel to Popwell's gambling den "to buy large quantities of change, which Popwell stored in 55-gallon barrels in the basement." Still, on any given gambling night, there was often as much as "$1,000,000 spread over his tables" ("From the Vault...").

Born on June 1, 1912, Popwell grew to stand five feet six inches and weigh well over 300 pounds. In 1996, thirty years after his death, he was voted into the Poker Hall of Fame ("From the Vault...").

§

**Should I Stay or Should I Go?**

Life gets curiouser.

That *Poker News* story listed Little Man's dwelling as being in Leeds, Alabama, a suburb of Birmingham. I ask my mother about this.

"No, it wasn't in Leeds," she says. "It was somewhere in Shelby County."

Sometimes hard work pays off to the diligent, and sometimes the diligent get lucky. Sometimes we hit our very strange number, and though a "3" in craps is..."craps," three's are important to the location of Little Man Popwell's gambling joint.

When I Googled "Leeds, Alabama," naturally my first hit was Wikipedia's entry. View Wikipedia with suspicion all you want, but this entry solved the mystery:

"Leeds is a Tri-County Municipality located in Jefferson, St. Clair, and Shelby counties," although it is principally a part of Jefferson County.

Leeds' more famous citizens are former Auburn and pro basketball star, Charles Barkley, and former Major League pitcher, Dixie Walker.

Sadly, Wikipedia fails to mention Julius Oral "Little Man" Popwell.

My mother describes Popwell's place as being "in the middle of nowhere." Roughly 11,000 people reside in this nowhere-land, according to the 2010 census, less than that during Little Man's run.

I am intrigued, though, by the "Florida Short Route" moniker. Where have I heard that name? It seems that my daddy used to call some road the Florida Short Route. Again, I ask my mother:

"Oh yes, I know that. It's the old way everyone used to take to Florida, before the interstates. That's highway 280."

US Highway 280 begins in Birmingham and travels south through Shelby County and on down. It's a major corridor into what was termed in the 1970's, "Alabama's fastest growing county." Much of Shelby's growth, if you consider the date the term was coined, was due to "white flight." Regardless, I remember my father's pointing the route out, and when he did so, all I could imagine was that if we could just drive over the next hill, I'd be able to see the beach. I assume that we did take the Florida Short Route on our trips to St. Petersburg. I have no memory, however, of the Alabama part of the route, except for random thoughts of the gas stations we might have stopped at to fill up, to release, to drink "Co-Colas" and eat cheese crackers.

So next, I Googled the Florida Short Route:

Before interstates and four-lane highways, U.S. 280 was the quickest drive from Birmingham to Florida's beaches and the only route to outlying areas such as Chelsea. The winding road was so traveled by sun-seeking tourists it earned the lasting name of Florida Short Route, as denoted by a billboard from a Tallahassee motel that pointed 287 miles south.

A branch of U.S. Highway 80 and running 390 miles from downtown Birmingham to Blichton, Ga., the route branches off to go south and east through Georgia to Florida's Atlantic coast. Still today, U.S. 280 south of Birmingham shows up on road maps as Florida Short Route.

In addition to being the quickest way to Florida, early U.S. 280 was the only route to Birmingham for residents in Chelsea, Columbiana and other nearby towns.

'It seemed like it took hours to get to my grandmother's house,' recalls Sandy Crumpton, the Shelby County Historical Society's archivist, who grew up in Columbiana and remembers riding through the famous 280 Narrows and over the mountains to Grandma's house in west Jefferson County.

The Narrows, the picturesque Yellow Leaf Creek gorge section of the old highway, had nicknames including 'War Eagle Highway,' as it leads to Auburn University, and 'Blood Bucket Road' because of the accidents on the narrow roadway, said Bobby Joe Seales, president of the Shelby County Historical Society.

Many vehicle accidents occurred on the Narrows' winding curves, and its hills and hollows hid whiskey stills back when store-bought liquor was forbidden or too far away. *Reportedly, a gambling casino was once located along the Narrows, Seales said* (Italics mine). Historians from half a century ago also reported that the rocks in the Narrows were the oldest found in North America at that time (Jackie Romine Walburn, "The short route to Florida," 280 Living, July 29, 2014, http://280living. com/people/the-short-route-to-florida/).

Whiskey stills, hollows, and a gambling casino. I saw none of those on our trips to Florida when I was a boy. I didn't know then just what I was looking for.

But I wonder now if my dad did? If, when he pointed out this route and drove on it, he remembered or thought of Little Man's place? If that

Saturday night in 1953 stuck with him—the fact of his mother's gambling, the nearness of his and my mother's arrest? While he seemed amused by his mother's love of all gambling games—and she had weekly canasta, pinochle, and bridge games with the cronies in her apartment complex— and while I remember his saying that she liked to gamble, he never told me about this casino night. Neither *how* he felt about it, nor *that* he went there at all.

Nor did he ever tell me his thoughts about MaMa's gambling away her grocery or rent money.

The one lament he spoke of was that while he was in World War Two, fighting the Nazis in Patton's Third Army, MaMa hocked his clarinet and used the funds to go gambling. She sold his comic book collection, too, but losing the first issues of *Action* and *Detective* didn't bother him as much as losing his precious clarinet, whose sound he duplicated the rest of his life with his own whistle.

I can never know how much this, or anything MaMa did, bothered him. Such are the stakes of loyalty. So very high, and costly. So secretive. And so eerily quiet.

§

**Loyal Restraint**

I got the details of my mother's trip to Little Man's as we drove home from The Greenbrier. I admit that I had fun, that rolling dice had its definite highs. But these are superficial moments, far different from the ones I truly love: hearing and telling the stories of our lives. My family is trying to keep me from revealing certain salacious tales. They'd like me to swear that I won't reveal sensitive details about them.

But I can't swear to that. Actually, giving up gambling would be easier.

I am pleased that my mother thoroughly enjoyed her weekend at The Greenbrier; she finally got to stay in the posh resort of her dreams. Clearly, though, my grandmother's action--her distorted self-absorption and her gambling--so long ago, still gives my mother nightmares.

And gambling is still illegal in Alabama, at least concerning casinos, craps and poker tables, and, it seems, gas stations where just yesterday in Lauderdale County, thirteen people were arrested for operating illegal gambling machines and "...more than $40,000 in the 128 machines [was] seized...in a 24-hour period" (http://www.tuscaloosanews.com/news/20180510/13-plead-guilty-to-operating-128-gambling-devices).

Despite this incident, you can bet on any major sporting event in the state as long as you know whom to speak to (in the 1970's, it was a beloved neighbor who worked at that same Bessemer liquor store of the apricot pound cake incident). We bet college football parlays in the 1970's, too. My dad paid a dollar on these occasions, and once, he correctly picked nine out of ten games, against the spread, and won $20.

There is also the dog track in Eutaw, Alabama, which has been there since the early 1970's, and which also houses other wagering games; somehow, betting on greyhounds doesn't seem to bother anyone, as if something legitimate is transpiring, as if we're promoting good wholesome fun.

Fun.

I think now about The Narrows, that twisting stretch of county road to Little Man Popwell's, "where many vehicle accidents" occurred, travelled late at night by three people I loved, one of whom at least had been having fun at the expense of the others. Despite MaMa's losses, on that night they truly were lucky.

For what if my parents and MaMa had gone to Little Man Popwell's a week later and been arrested? Where would they have been taken? What would have been their fines, and what would have happened to their reputations? My father's job? My mother's place in Bessemer "society?"

Furthermore, since MaMa was the instigator, had they been caught, would she have paid the fines for all three of them? Since she "knew people," could she have wormed her way out of being arrested? And if so, would she have tried to get my parents off, too? Or just my dad?

Or finally, just herself?

Would her loyalties have run deep enough to protect those who loved her, or at least tolerated her, or would she have hedged her bets as closely, exclusively, and selfishly as possible?

My son-in-law Taylor says craps is the game where the players have the greatest odds of beating the house.

So knowing that, knowing that craps was MaMa's favorite game, I'll go ahead and bet anything that loyalty to the "house" or anyone living in it was never her chief concern. She bet against it all her adult life. So I'll even double that bet, for I understand the terms of it now. She would have sacrificed all in order to get what she wanted: a good time, her son's singular loyalty. After all, it was just for a thrill. It was just a game of chance.

There is one last life irony in this story.

MaMa lived by herself until she was ninety-eight years old. Finally, she couldn't take care of herself any longer, and she had run off every live-in aide my dad hired, accusing many of stealing from her. So he moved her into a "home," Plantation Manor, out 4th Avenue, on the old Tuscaloosa highway.

In Bessemer, where she died the following year just two months short of her 100th birthday.

# Moose Park

She walked in to my office, like she was walking onto a stage, which made sense given that she was a performer, a concert pianist, at her young age. She wore splints on both forearms, from the wrists to three-quarters up the elbow.

"Carpel tunnel syndrome," she said, before I could ask.

She sat down across from me, ready to interview for an academic scholarship at Presbyterian College. We had twenty minutes together, and though we spent the allotted time, I remember only these things: she played well enough to work with orchestras and give city recitals; she had high cheekbones, feathered brown hair, was tall and could have been a beauty queen.

And she was born and raised in Forsyth County, Georgia.

This was winter, 1989, and Oprah and Hosea Williams, and hundreds of peaceful demonstrators had been and gone from Forsyth for a year. Oprah had filmed her TV show from the county seat, Cumming, where among other testifiers, she heard this from a longtime county resident:

> 'I lived down in Atlanta...it's nothing but a rat-infested slum...They don't care. They just don't care.' Asked if he meant 'the entire black race,' the man said no, 'just the niggers.' When Winfrey raised an eyebrow and asked, 'What is the difference to you?' the man offered to help her understand the distinction. 'You have blacks and you have niggers,' he said. 'Black people? They don't want to come up here. They don't wanna cause any trouble. That's a black person. A nigger wants to come up here and cause trouble all th time. That's the difference.' Many in the audience applauded as Winfrey lowered the mike to her side and simply stared into the camera (Phillips, *Blood at the Root* 229-30).

I knew that the Klan had marched recently in Forsyth, and I knew that it had brought national attention on this county, which was only two hours south of my home in upstate South Carolina. I knew things there were bad, but I didn't know how bad. So when I asked the young woman sitting before me—who was hoping that I would give her high enough marks to increase her chances of getting a full scholarship (worth about $140,000)—what it was like to live amidst the tensions and troubles of Forsyth, she looked at me quite placidly and said,

"Well, it's the media that have blown everything out of proportion and caused all this trouble. Yes, the Klan marched, but it was no big deal. It's really a good place to live."

Okay, what did I know about her home county? I'm originally from Bessemer, Alabama, itself once home to one of the most violent Klan chapters in the South. I grew up in the George Wallace era, and I wouldn't want anyone judging me or my intellectual capabilities based on Bessemer or Alabama in general. I wouldn't want any outsider believing that Wallace and the Klan's vitriol against the Black race defined me or my family and friends. So we moved on to other topics. In the end, I gave her a decent recommendation, but not the highest. I don't know if she was offered any sort of scholarship or what else happened to her that day or any other day. However, she never enrolled in our college.

Though I didn't believe her when she tried to minimize the effects of her home county's racial intolerance, I didn't know until I read Patrick Phillips' account of Forsyth, *Blood at the Root*, that the county went further than merely lynching black men back in the early part of the 20th Century.

It cleansed itself of all black people, a cleansing that held from 1913 to the early 1990s.

Reading Phillips' study, I learned about a world I thought I understood, being, as I said, a native southerner who has lived in the shadow of race my entire life. For eighty years, no black person set foot in Forsyth County without being run off, shot at, stoned, and I don't know, nor does anyone else, how many were actually killed.

Over the decades since our brief time together, I have often remembered that young woman. I especially think of her each winter when scholarship day rolls around. And last fall, when I read *Blood at the Root* for the first time, I thought of her again, especially when I got to a passage quoting Forsyth County Commissioner David Gilbert in 1987. The first peace march to protest the county's segregated life had just ended with the marchers being jeered at, threatened with bricks and guns, and then urged by the local police to re-board their busses because their lives could no longer be protected from the gathered white mob that was ready to do anything, it appeared, to keep Forsyth County racially pure:

> Gilbert claimed that the men who'd attacked African American peace marchers were all from outside the county—despite the fact that seven of the eight men arrested [that day] had Forsyth addresses. 'The real thing that upsets me,' Gilbert told reporters, 'is that this whole thing was sprung by outsiders. It's just a bunch of outsiders trying to start trouble in Forsyth County' (Phillips 70).

Forsyth had claimed for eighty years that it was outsiders, people living in other, nearby counties, who had caused all the trouble; who had forced black landowners out of their homes and out of the county. The law of Forsyth County thought, when it lynched two black men—one of them, a boy of fifteen—back in 1912 for attacking and killing a young white woman, that it had solved the crime, though another attack with a similar MO occurred *after* these two were already in custody. The true culprit was never brought to justice, but what did occur in the years just after the lynching was that a concerted band of night riders terrorized and ran off the black people of the county and some of the whites who sympathized with their fellow human beings. This band would eventually organize itself into the second wave Ku Klux Klan, and its descendants were dwelling in all-white Forsyth six decades later. And according to news sources, proud of it.

As I keep thinking about these issues, I wonder what that young woman saw and heard in her Forsyth years. Did she truly believe that her home was a healthy one, a peaceful one—one that practiced the standards of freedom and justice and Christian goodwill to all? That the races must be separated according to scripture or some other distorted idea? When we spoke, was she protecting others' views—the views of people she loved, those of the family she was born into? Was she succumbing to neighborhood peer pressure? Her story, her defensiveness, her reaction still haunt me. I understand her conflict, her defensiveness. I know the shame and rationalizing that come from seeing your hometown's name in cold brutal print.

§

As I write this, two days ago a white man named James Harris Jackson, from Baltimore, murdered a black man, Timothy Caughman, in New York City, using a military-type sword. The murderer told the police that he "has hated black men since he was a kid" and is "particularly offended" by black men sleeping with white women. The attorney for the murderer stated that if the charges and statements by his client are true, then he has "obvious psychological issues." Jackson told police that if he hadn't been caught, he would have kept on killing. The New York prosecutor is considering whether, along with murder, to charge Jackson with an act of terrorism (Kleinfeld, "A Man Who Hated Black Men Found a Victim Who Cared for Others," *New York Times*, March 23, 2017).

Along with my horror and sadness upon reading this story, I'm transfixed by the defense attorney's simple statement about his client's "obvious psychological problems." I don't disagree. Blind hatred of black men, a lifelong hatred, is a sign of sickness, of someone who has been damaged either intentionally or perhaps unintentionally. We know that such hatred is learned behavior. White men are not born with a natural, organic hatred of black men. White men are not born with an instinct to hate black men who especially want to be "with" white women. Such thinking seems a vestige of the past, something we shouldn't expect in our "post-racial society."

My problem, though, is that I was born in 1956, raised in Bessemer, Alabama, a suburb of Birmingham, during the Civil Rights years. Thinking about the case in New York today, my question is: where were the attorneys in my home state, my hometown, to publicly proclaim that the city fathers who directed our lives--the neighborhood fathers who pumped our footballs, who handled our bank accounts, who stewarded our church, or who sold us our furniture--be arrested or institutionalized because, given their views and teachings about the Black race, they themselves were "obviously psychologically problem[ed]?"

This semester I'm leading a seminar focusing on Southern Political Literature. My students have read *All the King's Men,* which we discussed in relation to the rise of our current political leadership. Then we turned to Lawrence Leamer's *The Lynching,* which recounts the Alabama KKK's hanging of a young black male, Michael Donald, in the early 1980's. Leamer provides a historical context for the brutal murder, showing Klan activity back in the 1960's, and particularly focusing on the Klan reaction to the March on Selma, the *second, successful* march. Reading this harrowing story, I reach the passage where Leamer describes Imperial Klan Wizard Bobby Shelton's appearance at Birmingham's Eastview Klavern #13, one of the most violent Klan chapters in the country. Present on this evening was "The next most important person at the meeting...Exalted Cyclops of the *Bessemer* Klavern and the Grand Dragon [or] top UKA officer in the state," Robert Creel (Leamer, *The Lynching,* 173).

For much of my life I have known that there was a Klan presence in Bessemer. My mother has told me often of the sign on Bessemer's "Super Highway," US Highway 11, leading from Bessemer to Birmingham, at the city limits next to Civitans and Lions and Rotarian signs: the one that welcomed everyone to Bessemer on behalf of the United Klans of America.

"It was just a small sign," she says, "maybe even hand-painted. It was right next to one of those train trestles out there. I don't know how long it stood or when it was taken down, but it was sure there a while."

While to my knowledge I never saw that sign, I have seen photographs of a Klan march right through the main artery of downtown Bessemer, 19th Street. The photo is somewhere in Bessemer's Hall of History today.

Also on the 19th Street of my boyhood, next to a Pure Gasoline station owned by Mr. Bradley who used to pump my mother's gas and who often gave her a "dollar's worth" when she could only afford fifty cents, was a barbecue joint run by an old, trembling white man whom everyone called Pop Green. I went into this place only once in my life, when I was a junior high kid, with friends who wanted a sandwich. I had no money and maybe one of my friends bought me a Coke. It doesn't matter, though, and maybe this fact doesn't either. But on the slightly faded neon sign out front, the place was not called Pop Green's or even just Green's.

It was Creel's BBQ.

There could have been many Bessemer Creels, though. I have asked a few people if they remember this sign, but so far, it seems it's only my memory.

I reported all of this to my students, asking if they understood how strange it feels to know certain facts that no one else remembers; to know secrets through hearsay and gossip but to finally see them being revealed in print—secrets connected to your hometown and to the Klan. And how strange it is to wonder not if you knew any Klansmen, but rather, how many you might have known.

"I know what you mean," one of my students responded. "I've lived in Forsyth County my entire life. I knew there was racial strife in the county's past, but it looks like any other town, now. There's even a Starbuck's."

Another sort of branding.

We all looked at each other then, wondering.

§

And then it got stranger.

On pages 141-2 of *The Lynching*, Leamer refers to a KKK rally in Bessemer on Saturday night, May 11, 1963. Imperial Wizard Bobby Shelton spoke at this rally, and later that night, some of these same Bessemer Klansmen participated in the planning and bombing of the AG Gaston Motel in Birmingham, hoping to kill one of the tenants, Dr. Martin Luther King, Jr, who fortunately wasn't in his room at the time.

1963 was such a year. Just a month after the KKK rally, Governor Wallace stood in the University of Alabama schoolhouse door attempting to keep the campus segregated. Four months after this bombing, another, larger bomb would go off in the basement of the 16th Street Baptist Church in downtown Birmingham, killing four black children. Two months after that, President Kennedy would be assassinated in Dallas. I was only seven then, but I was very aware of the President's assassination and funeral; however, I have no distinct memory of the day those four little girls were killed at all.

Nor do I remember that in my hometown of Bessemer on an almost summer night, 2500 people gathered for a Klan rally.

But maybe 2500 people didn't attend the rally, as Leamer said. For according to a reporter at the scene writing for the *New York Herald Tribune*, there were about "200 hooded and gowned men on hand, and about 900 to 1000 spectators in street dress" (Portis, KLAN MEETING DULL, IN SPITE OF CROSSES, *The Birmingham News*, May 13, 1963, 25). The reporter would go on to write other articles about the Civil Rights actions in Birmingham and throughout the South. He would later write a few novels, the most famous of them, *True Grit*. However, Charles Portis's story on the Bessemer Klan rally was a curious one.

The headline, proclaiming the rally "DULL," was funny enough. Portis elaborated in the opening paragraph:

A Ku Klux Klan meeting, for all its cross-burning and hooded panoply, is a much duller affair than one might expect. The hooded Klan rally here Saturday night—just before the bombings in Birmingham—limped along for three hours of nothing but Kennedy jokes and invocations of divine guidance (25).

The rest of the story drips with sarcasm and Portis's brand of semi-sarcastic, down-home Southern yarn-telling charm. He speaks of the "honored guests…the grand dragons of Georgia and Mississippi," and ends the account with this almost whimsical detail:

By 10:30 p.m. one of the crosses had collapsed and the other was just smoldering. Everyone drifted away and the grand dragon of Mississippi disappeared grandly into the Southern night, his car engine hitting on about three cylinders (25).

Reading Portis's story caused me to want to see who else had accounted for this rally. So I hauled down Diane McWhorter's *Carry Me Home* from my top study shelf. In research taken from FBI and secret informant files, she goes into greater detail, including the barbecue and beer at this, "the first Klan rally in North Alabama in some eight months," as well as the speeches from Shelton and others. And then she suggests that the menacing words of "bluegum niggers," and blessings on Wallace and Birmingham Police Commissioner Bull Connor, reached *several thousand* pairs of ears that night (McWhorter, *Carry Me Home* 425-6).

Of course, nothing much was whimsical, but everything was pretty vile on this night in my hometown, whether the crowd was 4000, 2500 or just over 1200. Perhaps worse, on the same Monday that Portis's story was published, *The New York Times* folded the Bessemer KKK rally into the larger story of the Gaston Motel bombing and its aftermath. The *Times* headline, though, is curious: "50 Hurt in Negro Rioting After Birmingham Blasts" (Sitton, May 13, 1963, http://partners.nytimes.com).

Curious because back then it was the rioting, not the bombing, that the powers-that-be considered more pernicious.

I don't want to debate journalistic bias, however. What truly intrigues me about these stories is their stated location of the KKK rally in Bessemer. Portis claims that it was held "...in a well-kept little roadside park, a gift to the city of Bessemer from the Loyal Order of Moose. Moose Park, they call it" (25). The *Times'* writer, Claude Sitton, however, reports that the rally occurred "...in Moose Lodge, on the city's outskirts near suburban Bessemer [sic]" (Sitton). I've checked other documented sources, and "Moose Park" seems to be the consistent, designated site. McWhorter calls it Moose Park, too (McWhorter, *Carry Me Home* 425).

This is fine, except as a native of Bessemer, I have never heard of Moose Park, nor can I determine if Bessemer's Moose Lodge existed or where it was.

I have asked not only local Bessemerites including my mother, but I have also checked with the Bessemer Public Library, the Birmingham Public Library, and the Birmingham Civil Rights Institute.

No one knows where Moose Park is, or if it ever existed.

But if it didn't exist, where were Charles Portis, Bobby Shelton, and the grand dragons of Mississippi and Georgia and Texas standing on that May night, fifty-four years ago? Were they in Bessemer, or on the outskirts? And if they were within the city limits, how close or far away were they from my family home?

Wherever it was, what in that park's atmosphere carried through town? What did we all breathe in? What metastasized in our systems causing us to either hate or ignore our fellow men?

So far, no one that I know of except me seems bothered by this missing park.

I ask on the "Fond Memories of Bessemer" Facebook page if anyone remembers Moose Park, or Bessemer's Moose Lodge. People keep telling me that I must mean the Elks, and I assure them that I know the difference:

"Everyone knows where the BPOE (Benevolent Protective Order of the Elks) club was located," I say. "It shared a building with a children's ballet studio where my first girlfriend Mary Jane and her sister Margaret Lou used to practice on Mondays and Thursdays. Right on 4th Avenue on the other side of Highway 150. But that wasn't the Moose club."

Another funny detail: McWhorter describes Bobby Shelton's speech at the Klan rally as having "the tone of a Lions Club meeting" (426). Why didn't she use the Moose for her reference?

People are quick to try to help. My childhood friend Freddy, whose father was a Shriner, but no Moose, sends me an article, but it's only a truncated version of the Sitton article above.

An old girlfriend, Vicky Vincent, someone I didn't treat as well as I should have back in high school, contacts the Bessemer Hall of History and another history source at Tannehill State Park. No luck.

"But I'm gonna keep trying, Buddy," she tells me. "This is fun."

If it ever did, Bessemer, I discover, no longer has a Moose Lodge, the closest order now being in nearby Midfield, chartered in 2010. I think of contacting that lodge, but the lead seems tenuous. I know that I need to go back to Bessemer, perhaps to look in old city directories in the library.

My friend Joe, Mary Jane's older brother, thinks Moose Park might be situated in the MacNeil area of Bessemer, and he offers to drive me there the next time I visit:

"We can find it," he says, and I feel reassured, though he doesn't remember anything about such a place, so perhaps this is just another reason for us to drive somewhere, an activity we engaged in frequently back in the old summers when we needed to escape evening TV.

Now, I'm even doubting my sources. Was someone feeding McWhorter, Portis, Leamer, and Sitton a line about the loyal Moose? But then, in Gary May's account of the Klan killing of Viola Liuzzo, *The Informant*, there it is again: the Bessemer KKK rally in Moose Park (May

339). What do all of these outsiders know that the rest of us who lived there don't?

Perhaps they know more than just the same Bessemer Klan members' names: Robert Creel, Eugene Thomas, and E. O. Eaton. May, at least, knows about events like Klansmen using chains and blackjacks wrapped in fishing line to beat black people at the 1962 carnival in downtown Bessemer celebrating Bessemer's 75th anniversary, the Diamond Jubilee. Reportedly when a Bessemer policeman discovered the beating, he called one of the Klansman (who happened to be FBI informant Gary Thomas Rowe), a "dumb shit," and told him to wait a minute. The officer then called another cop to take the Klansman to an area where six popcorn crates were being kept, each containing a multitude of "clubs, bats, guns," where the officer encouraged the Klansmen to store their weapons until needed:

"When the signal comes down," the officer advised, "you can take [the weapon] out of the popcorn box and do whatever you want to do," (May 61-2).

No one I talk to remembers this act of violence. They do remember that for the jubilee itself, our fathers grew beards and wore tasseled bow ties as throwbacks to Bessemer's founding age. I think I remember this carnival. The intersections of 2nd and 3rd Avenues at 19th Street were closed off. There were rides, maybe even a Ferris wheel. Joe remembers sawdust strewn on the streets, and I believe I saw this spectacle. But did I? Did my family take a chance during these troubled times of letting us have fun on our still segregated but increasingly dangerous city streets? I was only six then, and so whatever violence they learned of, I'm sure my parents kept it from me.

Also mentioned in May's book are Klan hangouts in our town: Lorene's Café and the Barn. I'm troubled by all these scenes, locations, stories, because until now, I have known little-to-nothing about them.

Until now, I have allowed my past to be sanitized by those who loved and protected me, and for too long I have participated in the sanitizing.

Now I want to know: where are these places, and where did the Klansmen live? How close were they to my family and to other people I knew? To what degree did they infiltrate my life? Will discovering these sites bring my world into focus? Will it allow me to quit apologizing, quit denying, and *own* my past?

§

Two men, former Bessemerites who are now prominent lawyers, read my first book, a collection of essays on growing up in Bessemer, and then contact me as I am researching this story. The first, Al Pearson, tells me a few of his Klan memories:

"One night I was heading to Birmingham with my girlfriend to go to a movie. Cars were stopped and a huge cross was being burned. KKK members were looking into cars. They let us pass but the scene was intimidating. It was on the Super Highway, just about where the old Wigwam hotel was."

Pearson also remembers that after the Liuzzo murder, the Klansmen who killed her returned to Bessemer, and on the street the next week, people were stopping the "Thomas guy" (Eugene Thomas) and "congratulating him on a job well done."

Al tells me he'll look into the Moose Park business and get back to me.

I also hear from Joel Dillard, a Birmingham attorney who practices in the same firm as former Alabama Attorney General Bill Baxley, the first prosecutor in Alabama to successfully obtain a guilty verdict on a Klansman—one of the vicious men who bombed the 16th Street Baptist Church in Birmingham, killing those four little girls back in 1963. Though also a Bessemer native, he's never heard of Moose Park. I hope to meet Joel soon to find out more of what he does remember about our town.

When I report all of this to my mother, who is still my main fountain of Bessemer lore, she tells me that, according to a good friend, the Klan used to meet regularly on the second floor of the EL Huey furniture store on 3rd Avenue. That building is still there, and as I relay this information to others, they think it's likely true, given Mrs. Huey's racist attitudes. I never knew the Hueys, nor did we patronize their store. When I see the old Huey building on 3rd Avenue today, I notice it's for sale. I wonder if the seller knows about the rumors of its history, and if so, if he'll keep that information under wraps until and even after a deal goes through.

There are other wonders on Bessemer's 2nd Avenue. From the 1920's through the 60's, Jewish businesses thrived. In fact, near where Klansman/FBI informant Gary Thomas Rowe beat a black man at the Diamond Jubilee carnival sits the shell of I. Rosen's, once a prominent men's store. My mother remembers how the iconic "Red Goose" for Red Goose shoes stood in the front window. Still today, but given Bessemer's rotting downtown core who knows for how long, you can see the marble-embedded I. Rosen letters on the front entranceway. What must Mr. Rosen, his family, and the other Jews of Bessemer have thought living in such violent Klan territory? Also on this block were Sokol's, Pizitz, Picard's, and Loveman's, all Jewish-owned businesses.

It was in Pizitz, in fact, that I first encountered the truth and fear of segregation.

I was downtown that day with my friend Carl and his family. I couldn't have been older than three or four, because, it seems to me now, I must not have been able to read yet. We were on the second floor near the elevator, and on either side of this elevator were water fountains, the kind attached to the walls, with silver levers that you turned to drink. I was at least big enough to tiptoe to the fountain, sure of my ability to reach the spigot. So sure, that while Carl drank from the fountain on the right, I never thought for a moment of waiting on him to finish. There was, after all, a perfectly fine and free fountain to the left. I can't remember now whether I got any amount of water through my lips, but let's say I did before this happened:

A yank on my shoulder. Carl's mother's face glaring at me in fear, horror, or maybe it was plain, unadulterated adult disgust.

"That's not your fountain, Buddy. Can't you see? That word right above you? It says 'colored.'"

And sure enough, Carl's fountain proclaimed, "white."

I know I wasn't the only one to run afoul of these codes. I know that my crime and shame were very minimal compared to what so may others endured.

I am no victim.

I also know that across the street from Pizitz was McClellan's, a five and dime store, which actually had two entrances. The main one on the 2nd Avenue side introduced shoppers to candies and sundries, and to a long soda/lunch counter where multi-colored balloons hung overhead. If you wanted a banana split, you could ask your server to pop a balloon, and then you'd pay what the little slip of paper that floated down from on high said. Maybe full price—35 cents—or maybe only a penny.

McClellan's was L-shaped, and so as you made the elbow-bend, you'd see more goods and another lunch counter which you could also access from the 19th Street entrance. I don't remember if this lunch counter had colored balloons above it, but of course I remember that sitting on its stools it had only colored patrons. This would have been true, of course, during the days of Bessemer's 75th celebration of itself.

Those carnival days.

Two years ago, my mother, my wife, and I walked into the former Pizitz building, which is now United Textiles. We wanted material for curtains as we had remodeled our living room, and my mother suggested this place as it had quality goods for less. We did find some very nice fabric, and I know I helped the search. But before I could join the shopping, I had to stand at the elevator again. It still functions, but gone are the water fountains on the sides. It's odd to stand there seeing my past, and if I didn't trust my memory so completely, I might wonder at the reality of modern times when we accepted a world in which hatred and fear dominated us all as we tried to go about our business in the downtowns of our lives.

Last week, in the course of a casual conversation about Alabama's latest disgraced governor, Robert Bentley, my friend Joe and I were remembering the segregation of our boyhoods:

"Here's something I never told you," he says, and I grow so alert that I think my wife in our bedroom can hear my adrenaline. "My grandmother and I were in Birmingham one day shopping. We were driving in her black Cadillac—you know she could barely see over the steering wheel—and up ahead, we were detoured from our street. 'What's going on,' I asked. 'Nothing,' she said. 'I'll talk to you about it later.'" He pauses a moment.

"What I saw was Bull Connor's police turning fire hoses on those children."

"Shit," I say, for what else is there?

I didn't see that kind of trouble; my parents quit taking me to Birmingham for a while during those months, and we also stopped going to "Kiddie Land," where black citizens picketed the park's segregated policies.

Another site comes back to me, though. Like most southerners, my family craved good barbecue, and back then, it seemed that that were real pit barbecue joints on every street corner of Birmingham and Bessemer. Among our frequent go-to places was Ollie's on Birmingham's south side. They sliced their pork and used a vinegar sauce unlike any other barbecue spot in town. What I remember most about Ollie's, however, was the sign outside: a globe of our world, North and South America featured, with the neon legend "World's Best Barbecue" emblazoned on it. Like the Ferris wheel at "Kiddie Land," I see Ollie's globe in my adult dreams.

Of course when I first remember Ollie's, it was segregated. Black people could come to the counter and order, but they couldn't eat-in. Most of the cooks and servers were black; many had been working at Ollie's for thirty or forty years. In 1964, the US Congress banned segregation in public restaurants, and Ollie's sued. Ollie's last name was McClung, and the case became a landmark in the Civil Rights era and in American constitutional law (McClung and Heart of Atlanta Motel vs. the United States). After the McClungs lost their case, on the very next day, civil rights workers entered the restaurant, and McClung told his staff to "serve them like everybody else." McClung had argued his right as a local business to serve whom he wanted and how he wanted. But when he lost, he complied peacefully, if not a bit begrudgingly (https://news.wbhm.org/feature/2014/ollies-barbecue-the-case-that-integrated-restaurants).

I ate at Ollie's often, and even after it moved to another south side location, I continued eating there, the last time somewhere in the 1990's. I spoke to Ollie McClung Jr. that day and asked him about the events that made Ollie's nationally famous. He spoke quietly, politely, but since it was a busy lunchtime, he seemed more harried than anything else. I didn't ask him how he felt about black people now, about the state of civil and equal rights in the South. He explained again why he and his father brought the suit, that they felt they were right. Ollie's still employed a mainly black staff, and as I looked around the jam-packed seating area, all of us, black and white, were enjoying our hickory-smoked pork.

Ollie's closed in 2001, and McClung sold his sauce recipe. You can still buy it by the bottle in area groceries, but I can tell you that aside from the globe-legend on the label, it isn't the same.

Of course most things change, but as Human Rights lawyer Bryan Stevenson reports in his memoir of practicing in Alabama, *Just Mercy*, there is a constant in this racial drama: the fear of racial intermarriage--Baltimore killer James Harris Jackson's motivating fear--which is the real reason for the legacy and persistence of segregation, white animosity toward blacks, lynching, and all that goes with these torturous acts and beliefs.

What didn't change, however, until the 21$^{st}$ Century, was an Alabama statute banning interracial marriage:

> In 2000, reformers finally had enough votes to get the issue on the statewide ballot, where a majority of voters chose to eliminate the ban, although 41 percent voted to keep it. [Moreover, a] 2011 poll of Mississippi Republicans found that 46 percent support a legal ban on interracial marriage, 40 oppose such a ban, and 14 percent are undecided' (Stevenson 29).

Knowing such facts, I keep wondering what the support for re-instituting separate water fountains would be? If I feel so scarred by being pulled away from legitimately pure water, what must someone who lived an entire life under such hateful policies feel when he or she remembers Bessemer, our hometown? Just as we have no choice in our parents and the home where we are raised, we have no choice in the town of our birth either.

A few hours after I write these words, I listen to the last episode of *This American Life* and *Serial's* new podcast, *S Town*. Writer Brian Reed travels to Bibb County, Alabama, the town of Woodstock specifically, just a half-hour or so from Bessemer. There he interviews and gets to know John B. McLemore who called *TAL* originally, suggesting that they might be interested in this place he calls "Shit Town." John has lived in Woodstock all his life, and I won't go into the details here (I've already spoiled an episode or two for friends by doing so), but Reed's commentary toward the end of this last episode haunts me.

Reed tells us about John's struggle with racism, a by-product of his living in this area. In the 1950's the KKK posted a sign at the county line claiming that "The Klan people of Bibb County Welcome You." Reed learns that Bibb County was the last county in Alabama to comply with the court order to desegregate its schools. That was in 1967, a year after Bessemer did so, and thirteen years after Brown vs. Board of Education. During the heyday of Governor George Wallace, citizens of Bibb County regularly voted four-to-one to keep the former Battlin' Judge in Montgomery. And the town of Woodstock itself is still 95% white, a product Reed attributes to decades of "laws, violence, and day-to-day racism."

I can attest that Bibb County is...quite rural. It sits between Bessemer (Jefferson County) and Tuscaloosa (Tuscaloosa County), which is home to the University of Alabama, the seat of winning football teams and the school where Wallace stood in the admissions door back on June 11, 1963. Perhaps Bibb County welcomed the exodus of white people who fled Bessemer back in the 60's, 70's and 80's. In any event, I wonder, as I

listen to Reed's near final words about John B. McLemore, how true they
might be of me:

> "So much of the stuff John said he hated about Shit Town—
> Harley's, tattoos, misogyny, homophobia, and racism—he said
> he despised it, but that stuff was part of him, too."

I know that if I don't look closely and fully at the scenes of my own
Shit Town, I won't be doing justice to anyone, including myself. I won't
be able to see, finally, that this history of my home is real. To make it so, I
must see where the seemingly forgotten moments of Bessemer's shaded
history occurred. I must go back and search.

So I do, and *this* is what I find.

§

Joe and I are crawling along the backstreets of north Bessemer,
looking for "Short 14th Street." I enlisted Joe's aid because he knows every
street in town, in the next few towns over, in our county—Jefferson—and
the surrounding counties of Shelby, Tuscaloosa, and Bibb.

We're cruising in his relatively new black Mercedes, not exactly the
unobtrusive conveyance one might want to use when stalking the houses
of former Klansmen. But it's what we have.

We pass "Long 14th Street," and I can't believe I never knew that
Bessemer's city officials were so OCD as to name streets in this manner
and to be utterly correct in their reasoning. I can't see the end of Long 14th,
but as we come to the next street over, Short 14th, I see that it is maybe six
blocks long. The two streets are entirely separate. We make a left, looking
for the street number I found that morning in a 1960 City Directory housed
in Bessemer's Hall of History.

"I think we have a problem," Joe says.

I see what he means. The numbers are running against us, or
rather, against I-59 just ahead of us.

"Yep," Joe adds, "the house you're looking for has been eaten up by the interstate."

"What are the odds," I ask. And then I think, "What the hell, I'll just take a picture of the street and the spot where Robert Creel, former Grand Dragon of the Alabama KKK, used to live. There's a strange justice in this."

Joe, though, doesn't give up.

"Never leave an uncertainty," he says as he swings the Mercedes back around. We make three turns going around and under the interstate, and sure enough, Short 14th appears again, the final block of its street life. The second house from the corner on the right is Creel's house, 1511 N. Short 14th. Joe pulls close and I take several shots with my I-phone. I see no one around. The house looks occupied, and I know if it is, the residents—not so strangely, given Bessemer's recent geography and history—are black.

'Thanks man," I say, unsurprised at my friend's persistence.

"You gotta always try," he smiles.

Yes, I think, especially when you're searching for men who ordered or at least set into motion the brutal slayings, fire-bombings, and overall acts of terror against an entire race of US citizens. Wouldn't you want to see where such evil dwelled? Wouldn't you want concrete realities as opposed to second-hand abstractions?

This discovery is one of several on this day, all revealed by my hour at the Hall of History earlier that morning.

When I walk in the Hall's front door, the able curator, Chris, asks if he can help me.

"Well, yes. I'm looking for information on Moose Park."

"You're about the seventh person to ask in the last two weeks," he says, shaking his head.

"Yeah, I know. I'm the one who got everybody started."

He smiles, "We've looked and looked but haven't really found anything yet."

The "really" in that sentence is more than a qualifier. It leads us to a backroom where Chris introduces me to one of the Hall's executive staffers, William Eiland. I went to junior high with William's brother Don, so we establish our connection.

"Yep, it's all set us to wondering, and we've looked through all our records and old directories, but we can't find any evidence or mention of a Moose Park or a Moose Lodge for that matter."

I think, "At least they have the directories here so I can look up other addresses: Creel, Eugene Thomas, Lorene's Café." William isn't finished, though.

"But I had an uncle who I know was a Moose. I remember that he and the lodge sponsored his daughter, my cousin Beth, in Bessemer's Christmas pageant back in the late 60's. The competition to crown the Christmas Queen. So I know there was a Moose Lodge."

He's right about that. Later I will discover in a copy of *From the Rough: The Bessemer Story*--the historical program published for Bessemer's 1962 Diamond Jubilee--under a list of "Our Fraternal Organizations," the "Loyal Order of Moose #509." It's strange, however, that I don't find an address for the lodge anywhere in the city directories, and I search from the early 1950's to the mid 1960's. Nor does Moose Park appear in these directories. Did the Moose not have a lodge, a clubhouse, or a hall? Did they roam the Bessemer hills? Or were they in disguise?

Other friends had vaguely remembered the Moose existing in Bessemer, but they hadn't offered any proof. Actually, William hadn't either, but he wasn't finished.

"Yep, I've checked into it, and I believe I know where Moose Park was. Out there on the Bessemer Super Highway, across from the old Holiday Drugs, there was a big open field, and in back of that field was a lake. I hear people used to go on picnics there. Later, next to the field, they built a car lot that changed owners a few times. But the field was big enough to be a park, and with that lake..."

He trails off here, but—and the best way I can describe this is to say what I'm about to say—my "Spidey-Sense" begins tingling. This is near, or maybe is, the area Al Pearson described when he remembered the KKK filling the highway and stopping traffic: the area near the WigWam motel where off to the side, maybe in exactly the spot of that open field, the Klan burned that enormous cross.

"There was a building back there," William continues, and Chris, who has rejoined us, confirms this piece: "It was like a silver metal barn," he adds. "And up there, too, was a café called the Blue Creek Restaurant."

"I really think this was the place that was Moose Park," William says. "I really do."

If so, then it was also the place of that Klan rally in 1963, the place that no one remembers but which hosted the rally Charles Portis described as "dull." We check the city directories again. The street listings run out at 33rd, well before the stretch of highway Eiland has mentioned.

One more bit of unconfirmed information. In *The Informant*, May refers to a nightclub called "The Barn," a place Bessemer Klansmen targeted because black musicians there were supposedly dancing with the white waitresses" (58-9). A new study of race in Bessemer, *He Calls Me By Lightning*, also mentions The Barn, which, in the 1940's, Bessemer police "ignored," allowing whatever vice taking place there to continue "unabated" (Bass 55). I did find The Barn listed in the City Directory, but the only address for it was "Bessemer Super Highway." The Klan didn't bomb The Barn, though they planned to, but did they later take it over? Was The Barn that "silver metal" structure? Could it have become Moose Lodge? Maybe that's unlikely, yet no one at the Hall of History or anywhere else remembers The Barn either. I feel like I'm in an episode of *The X-Files*.

For at some point, don't all invisible place references converge as one?

Weeks later, my son-in-law Taylor, a lawyer who, like me, relishes the chance for historical research, finds this tantalizing story about a late 1950's-60's Bessemer area proto-garage band:

In the late 50's, Dale Karrah gave Fairfield High School friend Howard Tennyson a bass guitar and said' "Here! Learn to play this!" Bringing in another friend, Bo Reynolds, this led to the start of a band called the Satellites – named so for the current news-headlined launch of the Russian spaceship called Sputnik. The band consisted of Dale, Howard, Bo, and a drummer Skeet. Skeet bought a new set of drums made by Premier Drums, and since the name Premier showed on the side of the drum visible to the audience, they thought it would be neat to change the band's name to "The Premiers". Their first gig was on stage at Fairfield High School. They also played the Hickory Pit and the Madison Night Spot on the Bessemer Super Highway...The Premiers were truly a 'garage' band – practicing in Pat's garage on 41st Street in Fairfield. Bo would bring his records, and they would listen to a song over and over and practice learning it until they got just the sound they wanted. Pat bought an old piano and cut it down so he could carry it to jobs where there was no piano. They used it only a few times as it still weighed over 300 pounds. Pat remembers the gig at the Bessemer Moose Lodge located UPSTAIRS in an old barn on the Bessemer Super Highway. It took all of them to get that piano up the stairs that night, but it ended up being a great night as they played for over 4 hours and earned $5.00 each. They had so much fun while getting paid for it. (http://www. birminghamrecord.com/brc/hall_of_fame/the-premiers/)

Word places like "Barn" and "Super Highway" start popping up more often now. Was the Moose Lodge exactly where William thinks it is? Were it and Moose Park next to each other?

§

Back at the Hall of History, I ask William about another KKK hangout, Lorene's Café, 2200 8th Avenue.

"But that's in a black section of town," he says.

Yes and no. For in the Bessemer of those days, while segregation in public spaces was strictly enforced, the invisible lines drawn to designate streets of residence and even streets of business were never so indelibly or permanently etched. Lorene's, for instance, was near the Rolling Mill plant and Bessemer Foundry and Machine Company, and only three-to-four blocks from Mulkin Auto Parts, an establishment owned by the father and grandfather of one of my oldest childhood friends.

"Yes, but I've read that the Klan hung out at Lorene's," I tell William. "Can you imagine anyone in those days challenging where they went?"

Café owner Lorene J. Frederick is mentioned prominently in *The Informant* as one of the witnesses the prosecution called, attempting to link the time when Thomas and the others who killed Viola Liuzzo showed up in her café on their way back from Selma to Bessemer that fateful evening. Frederick couldn't pinpoint the time they arrived at or left her café, however. Or so she claimed under oath (213).

Joe and I drive over to 2200 8th Avenue. People still live around there, and the street abuts the former mill. I hop out of the car to photograph what had been Lorene's, and Joe chastises me for leaving the door open while the air conditioner is running. We truly experience first-world troubles.

Where Lorene's was--and God knows the planning, the debriefing, and the drinking that went on there—is now only a vacant lot, overgrown by the ubiquitous Johnson grass that is found in every Bessemer neighborhood. I wonder when and under what circumstances this infamous hangout closed and was torn down.

Enough wondering. It's time to find Moose Park, or at least time to believe it can be found. Joe and I pull up on the right shoulder of the Bessemer Super Highway, near the spot Eiland described. The former Holiday Drugs landmark across the highway is now Holiday Food Store, a disheveled convenience store, but I remember it from those old days, just as I remember that further up on the left were Kelly's Hamburgers, Paul's Park N Eat, and the Bama Drive-In. The site where we stop is vacant, the land extending back as far as I can see. Maybe there is still a lake back there beyond the weeds and grassy bluffs. I can't tell where a silver barn or any other structure used to be, but there is plenty of room for buildings and crosses.

I'm not sure what I feel, but I'm as sure as I can be, given what I know, that I'm standing in Moose and Klan territory. I look around, 360 degrees. It's a late April Saturday afternoon. Grayish clouds are forming, and later on this night a cold front will bring both rain and a twenty-degree drop in temperature. I look northeast, toward Birmingham, and think back to that night in May, some fifty-four years ago.

On many Saturday evenings during the year, my parents would take the Super Highway, going out to eat at Joy Young's Chinese Restaurant or Morrison's Cafeteria in downtown Birmingham. Then they might head to the picture show, the Alabama, Ritz, Melba, or Empire, to see John Wayne, Audrey Hepburn, or Jimmy Stewart in whatever imaginary fare was being offered. On other Saturday nights, we might drive this same road as a family to the Super Sandwich Shoppe, two miles past where I'm standing now, which, according to both of my parents, had the best barbecue in the area.

There were enough of these Saturday night excursions for me to realize that like Al Pearson, at least some of my family, perhaps with me in the car, might have driven past the forming of a rally, the dousing of a cross with gasoline, later to be burned. My father, a Jewish man, could have been stopped, threatened. So much could have happened. To my memory anyway, nothing like this occurred. I never saw men dressed in white sheets, nor did I ever see a burning cross. My mother doesn't remember seeing such either, and my father is dead.

Sometimes, though, he'd drive by himself to the Super Sandwich Shoppe for takeout. If he had seen these sights, would he have told my mother, and, if so, wouldn't she remember now? Or would she want to?

On the other side of the highway, right there in front of the railroad trestle, were formerly the signs welcoming travelers to Bessemer—signs sponsored by the Lions, Kiwanis, Rotarians, the Knights of Pythias, and Elks. And, reportedly, by the United Klans of America, and perhaps even by the Loyal Order of Moose. Though I take pictures, I don't need them to remember.

"Did you get what you need," Joe hollers from the car. "Did you take a shot across the highway?"

Yes and yes.

"What do you think," I ask him.

"I think there *was* something here," he says, though he explains neither the "was" nor the "something."

Another something gets confirmed a few weeks later when I read Jonathan Bass's *He Calls Me By Lightning*. At the beginning of chapter three, there is a photograph of the Bessemer Klan's welcome sign. It's clearly manufactured with a Klansman atop a white horse carrying a rebel flag. Below it, a handmade sign: "Welcome Bess. No. 20." The caption and the acknowledgment for the photograph say the sign was erected in 1959 (Bass 28). So far, I haven't confirmed when in 1959 the sign was actually erected, under whose initiation or authority it was built and placed. Nor have I discovered the date it was removed.

∫

We have one more stop to make: the home of Gene Thomas, who replaced Creel as the "Exalted Cyclops" of the Bessemer Klavern (May 119), the man Bessemerites welcomed with open arms after he participated in the murder of Viola Liuzzo.

When I find Thomas's address in the city directory, something that I dreamed/feared would happen actually did: his address was Fairfax Avenue, the street on which I grew up, where my mother's family had lived since the 1910's. The street number fools me at first; I think the Thomas house is to the west of ours in the "Jonesboro" section, still a white section. "Got it," I think and feel pleased with my discovery.

A few minutes later, I deflate: "No, that street number is to the east, in the black section of Fairfax." My family lived between 18ᵗʰ and 19ᵗʰ Streets, and beyond 19ᵗʰ, there was only one more block of Fairfax that, to my memory, housed white families during my youth. The directory, though, had noted that Gene Thomas worked at TCI—a division of US Steel—and this conformed to what I had read about him in *The Informant*. I tell my mother about my confusion, and she quickly affirms that, yes, white families actually did live that far down Fairfax. Joe agrees:

"Yeah, there were plenty of white families living down here back in the 60's."

I'm not sure how he knows, but his father was a realtor, and passed on to Joe knowledge of neighborhood divisions, of random facts about how Bessemer was laid out and zoned.

I feel better, and yes, I know that feeling better about confirming that a Klansman lived near my family is odd. Perhaps my joy is merely a by-product of successful historical research. I know, though, that this feeling--excitement, even joy—isn't strong because I *want* Bessemer to have been a violent place, not because I *want* the town and neighborhood I grew up in to be known as a Klan den. Rather, it's this strong because finding the evidence of where Klansmen lived, seeing how close I, my family, and many others I loved were to an active vehicle of race hatred and violence allows me to record in *this* moment that those *other* moments existed. Seeing what might have been Moose Park and, now these houses, allows me to write about them so that I and other Bessemer residents, other readers of this history, can see where we were in context and thus have the chance to face who we all were and weren't, what we did and didn't do, back in this time.

My research not only confirms all that I've read, it now enables me to see the living strains of history before my eyes; it allows me to enter the scene and see myself as a boy amidst friends and neighbors, not all of them racists and Klan sympathizers, but many who might have considered Thomas and his family good neighbors, good people.

Good because, perhaps *only* because, they were white people.

As a boy, I was told many things, some by my parents, some by others: to speak to a black kid only if I was spoken to first. That black neighborhoods weren't safe. That only white people, and not black, could be trusted. That only black people and not white could be violent, would hurt me. That segregation was the proper course. So many times when I went outdoors, I was told to be careful. I didn't know why exactly, and I never knew precisely that the fears put on me were largely based on race. But I did feel fear; I did feel white people's hate. I did know that there were "race riots" in places not too far away from me.

I didn't know, though, how close all of this was to me.

I know that anyone can be violent, can hate, and I know that some black people then committed violent crimes just like some white people were tolerant of integration.

What I'm saying is that my reality back then was distorted. I grew up being taught to trust one race and not the other when all around me there was evidence entirely to the contrary. There was no organized black violence against white people in the era of my boyhood, while white violence against black people, just like segregation, was entirely organized. I didn't see this reality back then; I learned this lesson only years later. But I'm seeing differently now, and now, back in Bessemer, I'm seeing clearly. Concretely.

And everything I'm seeing helps me understand that when my family told me to be good and that all was well, the feeling that I had—that all really wasn't well—wasn't unfounded or wrong.

The Thomas home is on the south side of the street at the end of the block, 2625 Fairfax Avenue. When we get to the right house, it is now--and probably has been for decades--occupied by a black family. One of the occupants, a black woman of roughly thirty, is sitting on the front porch. Joe drives on by before I can decide to photograph the house.

"But I didn't get a shot."

"Don't worry. We'll circle back around."

"I feel weird. I don't want to stop and call so much attention to what we're doing."

"Well, you could get out and ask her if she minds you taking a picture of her house," Joe says.

"Yeah, right, I can hear it now: 'Hey, I'm riding around Bessemer taking pictures of old Klansmen's houses, and guess what? You happen to be living in the grand prize of them all! Not only did a Klansman live here, but he was the Exalted Cyclops of the Bessemer Klavern and participated in the killing of Viola Liuzzo!'"

So Joe slows down to a crawl, and I stick my arm out of the window, snapping away without focusing and hoping that one shot will be what I need.

It's hard to make an outsider understand what I feel when I see this house. It is within walking distance from my old house at 1816 Fairfax. I walked further than this distance many times growing up on my street. Because I thought this was a wholly black neighborhood, though, I never walked down here. I knew, I was instructed, that walking east on Fairfax was off limits to me, though I also saw black people walking past my house every day, past my section of this street. Sometimes they ran, too, especially when one of us sicced his dog after them. But if I had walked eight blocks east back then, I likely wouldn't have seen anything stranger, or more threatening, than a white family living so near, even amidst, black families. Most likely, however, even if I had seen the house, I would have never known or considered this:

According to The *Informant*, when Thomas lived there, he had quite the gun collection: "...two pistols (a .38 and a .45), an automatic shotgun, three 303 Enfield rifles, a 30-30 Winchester rifle, two M-1 rifles, a Browning automatic rifle, a German automatic machine pistol, and hand grenades and blasting caps" (119). If that doesn't attest to the truth of Thomas's nature, this personal history casts an even darker light:

...Thomas had first been arrested in 1945 for public drunkenness.

Two years later he was charged with assault and battery, but the case never went to trial, probably because it was a domestic dispute—Thomas liked to beat his wife. He was again charged with the same crime in 1949, 1950, 1956, and 1963, with the added charge of carrying a concealed weapon (164).

He apparently threw the guns used to kill Liuzzo into the blast furnaces of the TCI plant that employed him (164). His ex-wife testified against him in 1983, saying that not only was he responsible for the Liuzzo killing but that he scared her and beat her regularly, though by this point Thomas claimed to have found Jesus (352-3).

Two blocks away from the old Thomas home, our family maid, Dissie, and her family lived. We drove Dissie home every day, and as Joe and I leave this section of town, I think about Dissie and whether or not she was aware of what lived so near her. But back then, I guess, violence was all around, and only my innocence and white privilege kept me from it.

A Klansman living in a sea of black neighbors. I couldn't have dreamed or invented such a scene.

Nor can I invent this one: as we drive away, we see a 30-ish black man walking toward us. His t-shirt is purple and gold, and as we pass I see that it says "Straight Out of Old Jonesboro."

"Hey," I say to Joe, "let's go back and ask that guy where he got his shirt. I think it's cool."

"Okay," Joe says, "but when we do, be ready in case I have to take off fast."

The sun has temporarily broken out on this early Saturday afternoon. The Alabama Crimson Tide is staging its spring game forty-five miles to our southwest, and I can't see a reason in this world why two grown white men in a black Mercedes can't talk to a black man on the roadside for a minute about his t-shirt without something so bad occurring that we'll need to peel away. But I don't say anything and let Joe pull alongside the guy.

"Hey man," I say, "I love your shirt. Where did you get it?"

He looks at us like this can't be all we want, can't be the reason we've stopped him.

He points kind of behind him:

"Aw man, it was just a party back over there somewhere, and they were givin' out these shirts. You know, just a neighborhood barbecue thing."

"You don't know where I can get one," I say.

"Naw, naw I don't."

We thank him and drive on. It's only later that I consider what he must have seen when we appeared.

"Old Jonesboro is the first part of Bessemer that was settled," Joe says. "I'll show you where."

He drives us to a section of town near the old West Lake Mall, an empty shell now on a site that used to be a gorgeous lake where dances, whites only, were held at its pavilion and where my grandmother taught me to fish.

Almost from its beginning, Old Jonesboro was a black section of town. I never knew its history or that it existed at all. I knew only of white Jonesboro--originally known as Fort Jonesboro and according to *From the Rough: The Bessemer Story*, the original "center of the new town" founder Henry Debardeleben envisioned--but that is just another case of my color-coded ignorance.

Old Jonesboro is now a few rundown houses, maybe two city blocks from that mall/lake, and roughly eight blocks from where Robert Creel, the Grand Dragon of the Alabama Klan, lived.

§

Even in the week since I've returned from Bessemer, when I bring up Moose Park people still ask if I can prove where it was, if it really existed at all. If you Google Moose Park, Bessemer, what pops up first is Debardeleben Park, Bessemer, which is a park in the inner city that is exactly one square block in size and named for Bessemer's founder. This threw me off for a while because I thought that Moose Park might be just another name for DeBardeleben, but no one ever knew it as such, and given the august proper name, why would they? Bessemer's other famous park, Roosevelt, doesn't come up on this Google search except at the bottom in "searches related to Moose Park." To fit the numbers of the Klan rally into Debardeleben Park would be nearly impossible, though such a crowd would have fitted Roosevelt, which is three-four times as large as Debardeleben. But Roosevelt was so central to Bessemer and so centrally located between white and black neighborhoods—it was the site of little league and Babe Ruth league baseball games as well as having the city's white junior high located at its western end—that if it were also the site of a Klan rally, enough people would have remembered. And given all the activity there (though officially Roosevelt Park was still segregated in 1963), some memorable friction or racial trouble likely would have occurred on that hot May night.

Something not likely to happen at a semi-unknown park somewhere on the edge of town.

Furthermore, the names of both of these more famous parks have been consistent all my life; no one ever mentioned an alternative name, much less one as noticeable as Moose. So I don't know what Google is up to.

Then I wonder: if what I found is Moose Park--scene of Klan activities and other, simpler pleasures--what happened to it? Why was it discarded, abandoned, almost literally thrown away and left to ruin or to revert to its natural state? Could it be because after the Bessemer Klansmen were finally brought to justice—not for murder but for violating Viola Liuzzo's civil rights—their infamous park lost its cache?

Sometimes in conducting amateur research, you forget the obvious. Almost at the end of my search, I think to call the Bessemer City Hall—the Clerk's office. I tell the clerk, Ann Benson, what I'm looking for—though not why—and she calls me back later with this information:

"The location of the Moose Lodge is 19th Street. That's all I could find, and I hope it helps you."

"There's no specific address?"

"No, just 19th Street."

This contradicts the article Taylor found on the garage band playing on the upper floor of a barn called Moose Lodge on the Super Highway, a road also referred to as US Highway 11. The day after I get this information from Ms. Benson, Taylor sends me the transcript of a radio program on Birmingham's Civil Rights era, produced by Pacifica Radio. The program, entitled "Freedom Now," features the voices of prominent figures of this era—figures on either side of the Civil Rights battle like James Bevel, Charles Morgan, Fred Shuttlesworth, former Birmingham mayor Art Hanes, and infamous former police commissioner, Bull Conner. In this section of the broadcast, Bevel, an ally of Dr. King, reads from a Klan broadside:

ANNOUNCER: Saturday afternoon at a youth rally held in the 16th Street Baptist Church, to begin the next item on the movement's agenda, the voter registration drive, the Rev. James Bevel read aloud a circular, widely publicized, that morning, and broadcast once over a local radio station. BEVEL (Reading.): The United Klans of America, Knights of the Ku Klux Klan, the Knights incorporated presents a public speaking, "White Citizens, Know Your Rights." The city of Birmingham, and the entire United States of America, which was created by your ancestors for your personal benefit is under attack. It is under attack by Jews and Negro Communist citizens! Two low races of mankind, the Jew and Negro, are trying and succeeding in their efforts to take over the country that your ancestors fought and died for. The Jew leaders have said, "We shall destroy . . . whether Americans like it or not." The Knights of the Ku Klux Klan rally will assemble on the grounds of the Moose

Lodge at seven-thirty, Saturday evening. **The Moose Lodge is located on the Bessemer Highway, Route 11.** The date is May 11, 1963. There will be parking for automobiles. Mongrelizers, beware! The Klan is riding again. (http://www.crmvet.org/info/bham63.htm)

Perhaps the other historians I've read—Portis, Sitton, McWhorter—had a copy of this Klan circular, too. Perhaps this is the way into Moose Park, the most direct entrance I'll find.

§

I hear from other sources that I'm onto something. A friend of a friend says that Moose Park was on the Super Highway, just across the street from Holiday Beverage/convenience store. Another text, Townsend Davis's *Weary Feet, Rested Soul*, mentions the May 11 Klan rally and "two twenty-five foot burning crosses" overlooking the proceedings held in "Moose Park in nearby Bessemer" (65). Is this corroboration or merely hearsay, a park or tract of land near a lake next to a Moose Lodgehall that for want of any other name gets called Moose Park and so becomes an unknown legend?

On some level, maybe it doesn't matter whether I have found the real Moose Park or not so long as no one disputes what happened there on that night in 1963 and on the other nights in the Civil Rights era. Of course, there are some who have always disputed this era, its reasons for being, its events and results, and the changes in our institutions and social fabric that it wrought. No proof can shake, much less change, the minds of those who believe that the races must be kept separate, that we can't live next to each other, with each other, and get along.

Or that one race is inferior to another—less than human. Indeed, segregation and Jim Crow laws were a way of ensuring that the Black race felt and was kept inferior.

As I consider where we lived then and what that might have meant, I think again of Dissie. What did she think when Klansmen beat black men at Bessemer's Diamond Jubilee carnival downtown, in open, plain sight, without anyone being stopped or arrested? Or when they drove so close to her house on their way home after an evening of drinking and plotting at Lorene's Café?

Of course, I could ask the same questions about my own parents. When those KKK members drove Eugene Thomas home on the night they murdered Viola Liuzzo and then hung out at Lorene's trying to establish a viable alibi, their most likely route would be up 19th Street, the main artery through downtown. They'd pass the church and elementary school I attended, and as they drove south, they'd also pass the mom and pop stores where I'd buy baseball cards and lemon ice cream. Then at Fairfax Avenue, they'd turn left toward the Thomas house. But if they had turned right, just three houses down on the right, they would have found me, sleeping in my own bed, dreaming or never dreaming about that other world so far away and yet so close.

Dreaming, though, gets you only so close to this world. I want to prove these truths of Moose Park because history is too important to guess at. At Presbyterian College, I also teach a course in Holocaust Literature, and I know that even when written down and verified, not all history is believed. Also, I worry that by focusing on a place that no one knows about, much less remembers--a place I can't prove ever existed, yet a place that is mentioned over and over by legitimate historians--I will be adding to the doubts and questions some have, or will have, about everything related to this time.

Despite my qualms, though, I have to know the details of what those in power did to intimidate others, how they condoned and advocated violence against others. Against Black people. I want Bessemer and its residents to acknowledge that we white citizens allowed such intimidation and violence to happen. That even if we didn't do the violence ourselves, we abetted it or abided it, because for all the years subsequent to this violence, too many of us either pretended it didn't happen, wasn't so bad, or did our best to put it behind us. In many cases, we left Bessemer itself. The scenes of our hatred were there and they were real. We shouldn't remember or tell these stories to provide catharsis, exoneration, or relief, but to proclaim the truth, the history of Bessemer, of ourselves.

I understand and accept that this history will give "us" doubts; that our faith in what "was"—the rights "we" had to go to separate but superior schools, clubs, and businesses--will be shaken.

Another clarity: I hear quite often that Bessemer's school system through the mid-1960's was one of the best in the state. Perhaps it was, and there is nothing so very wrong in believing that. There is more to the story, though. In *From the Rough: The Bessemer Story*, a section on the history of Bessemer's schools, written by then Superintendent of the Bessemer School System James O. Knuckles, tells us about the straitened economic conditions of that era, 1958-1962:

> State taxes have not been sufficient to pay Alabama's public schools the amount appropriated by the Legislature. The Bessemer schools, as an example, have been deprived of approximately $290,000 which the Legislature had appropriated. And yet, during this same short period, the enrollment in Bessemer has increased from 7336 to 7982 (Knuckles, *From the Rough*).

The increase in student population should have been a godsend for Bessemer; a thriving city should want to welcome the abundance of schoolchildren, black and white.

Yet, that wasn't the history of the Bessemer city fathers' reaction.

Perhaps Bessemer's citizenry didn't have enough time to consider its abundance, though, since it was considering other measures: fiery crosses; how to evade and delay the mandates of district courts; how to follow a new and even more segregationist governor.

Or maybe Bessemer's leading citizens, its white citizens, were living in the dream of Diamond Jubilees and racial purity. Consider the paragraph that follows Knuckles' account of the Legislative shortfall:

> In spite of the distressing financial plight, at the State level, the increase in enrollment, and the constantly increasing price of materials and services, the community can take pride in the achievements of an able and determined Board of Education, the Superintendent and a competent professional staff. Bessemer High School's overcrowded condition has been relieved and the Bessemer Junior High School is well established as a full fledged junior high school. Carver High School *has come on to the scene* [Italics mine] as the second Negro high school in the City (Knuckles, *From the Rough*).

Knuckles also lists the entire Bessemer School System later in the essay, making sure to cite which schools are for "Whites" and which for "Negros."

This was inscribed in 1962, eight years after Brown vs. Board of Education, and, again, the year of Bessemer's Diamond Jubilee. Over the week of celebration, including the violent downtown carnival, a pageant committee staged an historical drama each night at Bessemer Stadium. I know that the committee producing the pageant was entirely white, and in *From the Rough*, there is a listing of all those who participated in the pageant. It's a full page listing, and I'm guessing that 500 names are mentioned there. I'm also guessing—a reasonably assured guess—that every name corresponds to someone white, even though the majority population of Bessemer for much of its history was black.

Yet in another section of *From the Rough*, there is a history of Bessemer's religious community, and included there are its Jewish and Catholic congregations. Bessemer had a synagogue and a Catholic church.

Robert Creel, KKK Imperial Wizard, lived approximately six blocks from each.

Yes, there is more to Bessemer than just a black and white view. I know, though, that we shouldn't overlook the obvious, the real, or the forgotten places just because times have changed and people have moved on. In truth, Bessemer was a good place to live for many; even now, it boasts the oldest continuous serving restaurant in the state, The Bright Star. It was good to me, too, in that I was privileged and comfortable enough to be protected, taught, fed, and sheltered. In twenty years, the city will celebrate its 150th birthday, and whichever jewel commemorates that jubilee, I wonder what rough story Bessemer will tell about itself then. In any event, unlike the views of that student who enters my mind's office each January, I hope this story will give pause to anyone who believes or pretends that things in old Bessemer weren't as bad as they were portrayed by the media. I hope the details of Bessemer's history won't get further obscured, distorted, or lost. For this isn't only, or mainly, my story.

Moose Park is about all of us.

Postscript:

According to Moose International, "The Bessemer Chapter was instituted on 11/19/1961 and closed on 12/31/1964. Unfortunately, Moose International went computerized during the 1980's and all records prior to this timeframe are located on micro phish. Due to short staffing and the amount of time to review the micro phish information we are unable to provide location or reasons as to why the chapter closed. Typically, Chapter's close due to lodge closures, chapter's cannot obtain officers or lack of interest, etc." They also clarified, that this record is only for the chapter, not any building or barn where the chapter regularly met. The phone line to the Midfield/Fairfield office of the Loyal Moose Order is no longer in service. The leader of the Anniston chapter says he never heard of or knew that there was a Bessemer chapter, and he's "...been the leader here for twenty years." Maybe so. Anniston is roughly sixty miles from Bessemer, and so much can happen in the distance in between.

PPS:

Strangely disputing the Moose International's dates is this:

From the June 23, 1961, issue of *The Bessemer Advertiser*--a weekly paper published since the late 1880's—the Loyal Order of Moose, Bessemer Lodge #509, welcomed Judge George Wallace to its "recent grand opening." Welcoming Wallace, who was campaigning for Alabama Governor, were "Governor (of the Lodge) Bill Thompson, Bro. LC Deen, past Governor of the Gadsden Lodge, JW Abernathy, special events chairman, and several officials of the Birmingham and Ensley Lodges. Mr. Abernathy announced that one of the projects of the Lodge is the Little League and Pony League Ball Field [presumably in Bessemer's Roosevelt Park] which is almost completed and ready for ball games" [Information courtesy of Bessemer Hall of History. Gov. Thompson was Hall employee William Eiland's uncle, mentioned earlier]

First United Methodist Church, where "I Didn't Have
That" occurred. In the distance is the site of Arlington
Elementary, now just rubble.

The Fairfax Avenue former home of Klansman Eugene
Thomas (Moose Park) just six blocks from where I lived.

The former home of Klansman and Exalted
Cyclops Robert Creel (Moose Park)

The site of Moose Park, as best anyone knows.

GOVERNOR WELCOMES JUDGE—Governor Bill Thompson with Judge George Wallace at the recent grand opening of the Bessemer Lodge No. 509, Loyal Order of Moose. Judge Wallace was the guest speaker at this official opening by invitation of special events chairman, J. W. Abernathy. The Judge gave a very interesting talk pertaining to the high standards of fellowship of the Loyal Order of Moose. Present also were Bro. L. C. Dean, past governor of the Gadsden lodge and several of the officials of the Birmingham and Ensley Lodges. Mr. Abernathy announced that one of the projects of the Lodge is the Little League and Pony League Ball Field which is almost completed and ready for ball games.

Newspaper photo of Moose Governor Thompson shaking hands with Judge George Wallace in Bessemer.

Jane Mulkin, Carolyn Cummings, and my mother at lunch
at Birmingham's *Chez Fonfon* (owned by Frank Stitt).
Our last Birmingham lunch together.

My mother at *The Greenbrier* in West Virginia.
She had always dreamed of visiting there.
Her last trip before her passing.

# I Didn't Have That

I used to imagine the Holy Ghost as a fog that slept in the rafters of our church. I thought our music, surging, and shouting woke the spirit. When It looked down and saw us, It was reminded of how lonely It was, how much It loved the children of God. Like the wind, the Holy Ghost wasn't visible, but we could still feel Its power. It gave those It touched the ability to speak in tongues, the word of God pouring out of their mouths in garbled consonants and rolling vowels. This happens most often to men as they shout with their backs stiff and straight, their mouths a hollow that the Lord filled with song. --Ashley Blooms, "Fire in My Bones," *The Oxford American*, Winter 2017

My people were United Methodists, so docile and respectable that their rule was to stay quiet and thus reverent throughout the service even when the Black family who visited in 1970 showed up unannounced; even when they were escorted through the main and front left sanctuary door

just as the 10:50 am service was beginning (We began ten minutes before the hour so as to get a jump on the local Baptists and so beat them in line for seats at the best restaurant in town for lunch after Sunday service); and even when they proceeded to participate in the entirety of that service, opening the purple Cokesburys set in the back of each pew as we all did and singing "The Church's One Foundation" as if they really belonged here with the rest of us.

As if they were one of us.

They must have thought so, for just before the sermon, they even contributed real currency to the gilded offering plate that snaked through their and our midst, passed oh-so-politely by the church father-ushers in their vanilla suit coats.

Our church people took the "Black" money silently, but in the offices and back rooms afterward, or so I was informed later from my internal sources, our fathers truly united and hissed from their hollow throats the venomous words their own tongues formed from their own decidedly learned beliefs.

Still, I have to ask: was it the Lord, or Satan, or perhaps George Wallace who filled our men's voices?

Which of the three was it who caused our stewards to call to our preacher and help him understand that if he ever tried such a thing again, Holy Ghost or not, he would suffer not the little children to come to him, but the parishioners who would cast him and his wife out into the vacant lot of homelessness that really had materialized a couple of blocks down Arlington Avenue. He would be black-balled from Methodism itself, or so I heard, if he ever dared to welcome a Black family to church again.

Our fathers, as I read in the *New York Times* yesterday, were certainly not alone in their decisions:

> In 1958, the Baptist preacher Jerry Falwell, who would go on to found the Moral Majority, gave a sermon titled "Segregation or Integration: Which?" He inveighed against the Supreme Court's anti-segregation decision in Brown

v. Board of Education, arguing that facilities for blacks and whites should remain separate. "When God has drawn a line of distinction, we should not attempt to cross that line," he wrote, warning that integration "will destroy our race eventually." In 1967, Falwell founded the Lynchburg Christian Academy — later Liberty Christian Academy — as a private school for white students (Michele Goldberg, "Of Course the Christian Right Supports Trump," *New York Times*, January 26, 2018).

We started a segregationist academy in the bowels of our church, too. One of the early teachers was our preacher's wife. Someone, at least, learned her lesson. That academy moved after that first year to reconverted chicken coops in the western hills of town. These were, after all, the suburbs of Birmingham, circa 1969.

We were such a polite, servile congregation that the Sunday morning following the Black family's visit, we recited the *Affirmation of Faith*, the *Apostle's Creed*; sang the *Gloria Patri* and *Doxology* and some hymn I simply cannot remember; and collected another gilded offering as if the previous Sunday morning had never happened.

As if that day had been merely a blip, a momentary challenge to our order of worship, our collective appreciation of and voice to the Lord.

Our quietly reflective public voice to the Lord, spoken only in the responsive prayer portion of our service.

So no, my people didn't have what Ashley Blooms' people did. We never spoke in tongues, and would have turned away from the embarrassment had anyone in our Methodist midst, white or whiter, taken it upon themselves or, God knows, been filled with enough mystery to utter such spirit talk.

§

Despite our Methodist demeanor and my mother's stern warnings, I did the unthinkable once I learned to drive and could thus engineer my own dates.

I went out with one of those Baptists.

I've told this story countless times: how when I approached dating age, my mother blessed me to go out with anyone I wanted to (she herself had married a Jewish man), as long as that girl wasn't a Baptist. She might even have been more okay with my dating a pagan boy rather than a Baptist girl, for when my best friend "came out," my mother was one of his most strident champions. She had no worries about my sexuality, though I am likely over-assuming here.

Despite her strictures, my attitude toward Baptist girls was, "Why would I exclude any girl from any pool that would consider dating me?" My mother's religious biases were not my own. Of course, she never admonished me not to date a Black girl, since she never remotely considered that I would.

So when my first Baptist girl let it be known through a mutual friend—a friend who just happened to be the daughter of the First Baptist church's minister—that she'd appreciate my asking her out, I acted so cool.

I waited until I got home that afternoon to phone her, hiding in our darkened dining room to make this most important call.

We set our date for the following Saturday night. On that Friday night, our church decided to hold a lock-in for the youth group. The idea of spending a night in a cold, dark church didn't appeal to me, but whatever standing I had with my peers did. So I feigned as much excitement as an impious teenager could. On that night, though, nothing else about me was feigned: not my increasing nausea; not my getting sick in the basement men's room; not my having to be driven home by my friend Freddy, my shame multiplying with every step; and most of all, not the phone call I had to place the next morning, canceling my date.

Everyone else thought my sickness grew out of the frozen fish sticks that we gassed to death in the church kitchen oven. That notion made a certain sense and if true, would have left me feeling more or less sound on Saturday. Yet, I woke with a fever and couldn't keep any food down. I still wouldn't recommend gassing fish sticks, but what I had contracted was a classic adolescent stomach virus.

I could hear the mix of disappointment and disbelief in her voice. My Baptist girl later confessed that she thought that I simply wanted a way out of dating her. This was but one example of how well she didn't know me.

I convinced her to put off our date until the following Saturday night—that I truly was sick, especially over canceling our date. Finally the date arrived, and I remember that we went to the Green Springs Four Cinemas to see *Travels With My Aunt*, starring Maggie Smith. I didn't know then that the film was based on a Graham Greene novel, and truly, had I known, I wouldn't have known anything anyway. It was a strange movie choice and I still don't know why or how we chose it. What did it matter anyway, since ten minutes after the film started, we began making out?

After the film, we made our way back to Bessemer and to the parking lot up behind the Kingdom Hall of Jehovah's Witness building on 4th Avenue where, within ninety seconds, my date managed to remove both her and my pants in one decisive motion. And then, through our relative fogs, I heard her say,

"I'm on the pill to keep my periods regular. But I don't want to have sex."

Maybe my mother was afraid, then, of my dating Baptists because they were such fast movers.

In any case, I couldn't translate the tongue she was speaking in. I was sixteen, a good Methodist boy, thrilled beyond belief that a girl would kiss me this ardently and would be so kind as to remove my pants. So I considered this just an early stage of our relationship and decided to take her at her word. A few years later—okay, let's say a full decade later—it occurred to me that she was most definitely speaking a language that I translated badly, or really not at all.

Undeterred by my slow motion, the following night she invited me to do something else that I had never conceived of doing: she invited me to go to Sunday evening service with her at First Baptist Church. Why shouldn't I go, I thought? Isn't this what boyfriends do? Besides, how different could the service be from all I had seen and known at my own Methodist branch?

Very different, it turned out, as while things proceeded fairly normally for a time—hymns, offering, very lengthy prayers—there came a moment that we Methodists term "The Call to Worship," and which Baptists, I think, refer to as "The Time to be Saved." On this night, at this moment in the service, a high school boy I knew, Larry Turner, did what I had only heard rumors about before: he stood up in front of God and everyone and spoke in tongues.

Maybe he had the license to do so since he was our high school's junior class chaplain. Or maybe he was truly filled by the Holy Spirit and grew that hollow throat. I don't know, and the other thing I don't know is how to translate or approximate what I heard him say in the thirty or forty seconds that followed. Maybe he used words like "meshugge," "meghillah," "shibboleth," and "Cthulhu." Maybe he was speaking Russian, since our high school offered such a course.

Every kid I knew, most vocally Larry himself afterward, claimed that Larry went into a trance while speaking in the tongue of the Holy Ghost. I didn't know what to think, though my deepest suspicion was that he was faking. I don't know whether my date agreed or not, but I do know that when we walked out of that sanctuary, she suggested that we head back to the Jehovah Witness parking lot, where again, she moved in completely mysterious ways.

We spent a few weeks dating, practicing foreign-body maneuvers—maneuvers that never culminated because I wasn't sure what I wanted, much less what she wanted. And, I have to confess, her touch wasn't all that pleasant anyway. After all, what could she have known about pleasurable touching and caressing? She was only fifteen.

∫

"I was never filled with the Holy Ghost. Maybe I was too young. Maybe I didn't believe enough. Maybe I didn't ask for God's spirit in the right way. I didn't lift my hands when the choir sang and rarely sang along. I kept my body close, my hands gripped on the pew in front of me, my feet planted solidly on the ground. No toe-tapping, no bouncing... I wanted to dance like the others, but I didn't know howto unfold myself. I was afraid to be touched by the Holy Ghost" (Ashley Blooms).

I didn't have a spirit or body filled with the Holy Ghost, either. I have neither the conception nor the imagination of what that would be like. *Feel like.* To be touched by an angel.

Once when I was twelve, my church invited a youth minister from beyond our congregation to witness to my Sunday school class. This was so uncharacteristic of my church, perhaps of Methodists in general, but I suppose someone there knew about fast girls and parking lots. There must have been ten or twelve of us, many of whom were my good friends outside of church and generally scoffers and doubtful posers about any religious experience. The youth minister had us sit in a circle, him included, bow our heads, and then he suggested that there was one simple thing we needed to do if we wanted to be filled by the Holy Spirit and have eternal life:

"Just raise your head and meet my eye," he said.

At first, I wondered if such a thing could be real, but if being saved were this easy, why *not* do it? What could it cost? It didn't matter that I had already been Christened as a child, that I was a full-fledged member of the church with my very own Revised Standard Edition Bible, my name etched in gold on the cover. This was a booster, a guarantee. Supplemental insurance.

So I raised my head; I met his eye.

I don't know if anyone else did so because afterward in the safety of our walk to the nearby bakery, we all denied even thinking of doing so. None of us tough guys would admit to the weakness of wanting to be saved. Maybe we feared that the touch we would get from whatever spirit might be available to us might actually move us.

I don't know.

What I do know is what happened when I raised my head; when I met this twenty or twenty-one year-old minister-man's eye. I had never seen or heard of this man before. But I definitely saw him then, when he met my eye, when he winked at me. And when he smiled, only for me.

I looked down quickly, and neither in that moment nor in any of the millions that followed, through the rest of that "lesson," through the main morning service, or through our family's traditional Sunday roast beef lunch was I filled with anything other than the deepest sense of "creep-out."

I don't know how it is that a twelve-year old can know what he shouldn't know, what, if all else is good and equal, he shouldn't have to know. But in that moment, that time and place on the third floor of our church, I suddenly knew something I had never thought about before.

I don't know why the spirit of the Lord is so often coupled with forbidden acts or desires, though I've long sought these answers.

I thought of these scenes of my youth again, these uncomfortable, rebellious, and nominally religious moments, as I finished reading Ashley Blooms' essay, "Fire in My Bones":

> "I was afraid to be touched by the Holy Ghost. I was afraid to be touched. I was afraid that no touch could be good, because I had learned and was learning still that some touches hurt...What I can't forget: five-year old me, lying on my back on my abuser's cold basement floor, my breaths ragged as I stare at the place where mushrooms grow from the dark earthen walls. The stench of cold earth mixed with the mothballs scattered in the corners to keep the snakes away" (75-6).

I wrote my own ending of sorts regarding the Baptist church of tongues, maybe regarding the guises of supposed holy men, too. When I was seventeen, I was invited back to that house of worship by my high school choir teacher, who was also music director for the First Baptists.

I had been taking Choir as an academic subject ever since 7th grade, always with Mr. Fleming, our choirmaster. Who knows where he ranked as "effective," as "motivating," as "developer of young voices." Over the years he chose very strange arrangements for us: "Yellow Bird;" "Cantante Domine;" "When the Foeman Bares His Steel (Taranta-ra Taranta-ra)." He did try secular, popular tunes, too: "Raindrops Keep Falling on My Head;" "Windy;" "We've Only Just Begun." There was also some song about Noah's Ark where, apparently, some "animal" in dialect asked "Who dat Chevin'?" Our zenith as a choir, or rather in our offshoot "Boys Choir," was our performance of "Down in the Valley," for which we received "1's" at district competition and would have been invited on to state had some of our boys not been caught at the buses, smoking.

Poor Mr. Fleming. He tried so hard. In 9<sup>th</sup> grade he auditioned us for the spring musical, *The Pajama Game*. I have no idea what he or anyone else was thinking in 1971 about staging this musical. Most of my friends and I were listening to Santana, Led Zeppelin, and Jethro Tull; others to War, Stevie Wonder, The Temps. Yet, we also clandestinely admitted liking AM hits such as "Teach Your Children," "I'll Be There," and "Spirit in the Sky." The Youth in Christ group at school even hosted Religion Emphasis Week where, at the start of each day's assembly, someone would try to "rock us out," by playing "My Sweet Lord" or "O Happy Day." But they omitted, sadly, "One Toke Over the Line (Sweet Jesus)."

I tried out on a whim for the chorus of *Pajama Game*, but I never practiced beforehand and didn't realize that my audition song, "This Guy's in Love with You," was pitched too high for my voice. Fleming made me feel as good as any choirmaster could after my voice broke on the fourth line:

"Don't worry, I have a good sense of your voice," he said.

So while I didn't make the cast of that musical [Fred Kiker, whose voice wasn't any better than mine, did, because he chose a song that fit his range: "I'll Never Fall in Love Again"], Fleming didn't forget me, either. I got a short trio-solo in "Down in the Valley" when I was a sophomore. And then, in my junior year, Fleming took a greater chance on me.

I was in the choir at First Methodist, and our choir director, Mr. Pinion, would occasionally stage Sunday evening musicals for our youth. It was a no-brainer in the sense that at most, our Sunday evening service drew thirty parishioners. When we performed "Lightshine" at least we had a few more parents in the congregation. I don't know if Fleming heard about our success; one of the rival Baptist churches in town asked us to perform at their evening service, though we had to leave out any semblance of the choreographed square-dance number since, usually, Baptists and dancing didn't mix.

This is the point at which Ashley Blooms' story stops me.

In her Appalachian Baptist church, when the singing started, the women swayed and stomped their feet to the rhythm of the hymns. Despite all they had seen; despite all that had been done to them; despite the handprints on their arms. I didn't know that Baptists, especially women, could dance in church. After reading Ashley's story, I wasn't sure why they still wanted to—how they were able to pretend that what had happened to them hadn't, or at least, how they kept the faith to ignore what had happened or get beyond it.

I guess no one told the youth minister at South Highland Baptist about what was going on in the mountains above us, the dancing, that is.

However Fleming heard about our performance, or if he did at all, he remembered me. Staging a new religious musical for First Baptist, "Celebrate Life," he thought my high school baritone would be perfect for one of the three male leads. He also chose my co-Methodist best friend, a true tenor, and so "Go Methodists," right? So my innocent choirmaster let into the Baptist midst a closeted Methodist gay guy, and me: a boy who didn't believe in tongue-talk, and who had decided to never again raise his head to meet the gaze of a would-be spiritual host.

For three successive nights we danced (!) and sang in the Baptist sanctuary, and in the ironies of Art and Religion and Life's Great Celebration, my part allowed me to assume for one scene the holiest of Christian figures, writhing in mimed agony to the whipping perpetrated by the Romans just before they settled him for good.

I did the scene as faithfully as I could, and then sung along with the chorus, matching eyes with several earnest Baptist girls (none of whom being my fast date from the year before) who looked at me with a certain kind of fire, as the musical culminated with,

"**HE** IS ALIVE, HE IS **ALIVE**! HE **IS** ALIVE!"

I was never much of an actor, but in that moment, I understood the art of making others believe what you don't. What I can't.

§

But I can't leave the story here, because I can't let you think that I am unmoved by the sacred, or at least by sacred music. In the days when I went to church begrudgingly but faithfully, I sang every hymn that was ordered, whether I was in the choir or on the eternal back row of church youth. Singing was the only part of the service that ever meant anything to me. Even when I was a kindergartner not wanting to be separated from my mother, I stopped crying long enough to enjoy singing "In the Temple."

I didn't cry for love of spirit in church, though, and the hymns, as beautiful as they often were, never moved me to rejoice or ask to be "saved." Nevertheless, there have been two occasions when I have felt through sacred music something like a spiritual calling. They are strange moments, but then, isn't that how the Holy Ghost works?

There is an episode of "The Andy Griffith Show" where early on a Sunday evening, Andy and Barney harmonize to "The Church in the Wildwood," Andy accompanying them on his old six-string guitar. Maybe it's the peace of their voices, the nostalgia of the words. All I know is that I want to be on that porch with them every time I view that episode: "No place is as dear to my childhood, as that little white church in the vale."

The other moment comes in *Junebug*, the 2005 film directed by Phil Morrison. Centered on a North Carolina family and its prodigal eldest son, the film takes us one evening to a family night supper at the local Baptist church. The youthful preacher asks the son, George, to favor the collected with a song. George has apparently done this on many occasions in years past, before he escaped the church and his family. So together with two other sinners, he sings, "Softly and Tenderly Jesus Is Calling," to the tears and wonder of his mother, his sister-in-law, and his new outlier wife. I've seen the film many times and use it in my Southern Film class. Every time I show it, I have to turn my face from my students in this scene because they shouldn't witness their professor crying, especially over a hymn. Yet I do cry, and I wonder if it is only because of the refrain, "Come Home," or if it's more?

In these moments, I'd like to be sitting with George's family, and I wouldn't wince if the preacher came over and blessed me.

Still, that's not the same as believing. It's just not enough.

Is it, Ashley?

For even though I didn't encounter or experience your horror, or come close to your still-watered hopes, I nevertheless share your depths: "Maybe I was too young," and "Maybe I didn't believe enough," either. And you could say, couldn't you, that once I did meet the wink and the leer of a man whose tongue told me that's "all I had to do to be saved." I can fairly ask, then, am I saved or not? Is the intention good enough to countermand the actuality? But maybe I'm just playing with semantics, with hollow-throated and hollow-intended words. It's feeling the spirit that counts, right?

I think more about these moments today, when self-proclaimed religious people want to give passes to the powerful despite their violations of sacred, moral, and constitutional norms. Despite their refusal to denounce those who brandish hate with tiki torches or, yes, enameled or wooden crosses.

It's just like 1938 or 1967. Same as it ever was.

World without end?

And so, for whatever it's worth, I am the same, too, as I've ever been: that traditional spirit--Holy, Sacred, full of mystery--just isn't anything I've ever felt or had. Or truly believed.

# Imagine There's No Underwear

"I already knew what you were up to. Remember, I do your laundry."--"The Kids Are Alright"

Fill in this blank: "When I die, I want you to promise me that you will..."

No matter how you answer, I promise I won't judge you. I bet that whatever you say, though, can't top what my mother said from her hospital bed the week before she passed away from liver cancer.

Speaking of passing, it's hard to believe that it's been over three months on this side of her passing. I dreaded its coming for years—when a loved one hits eighty, people like me can't help counting—and now that this coming is in the rear view, I don't know how to feel. I'm not relieved except that she's no longer suffering. I'm still grieving, though my grief is no longer debilitating.

My good memories still shine, and though there are sixty-two years' worth to cherish, it's these moments from her last week that sustain and level me. They even make me smile.

I don't know what external or internal prompt pushed my mother to pronounce what would be her dying request. My wife, daughters, brother, maybe a good friend, and I were gathered round her bed. This was the night that my mother's oncologist had predicted Mom would leave us. Still, the hospice nurse that afternoon told us that she didn't think a passing was "imminent." Who knows what to think in such times? Any turn might take us all elsewhere. Yet looking at Mom propped in her bed, eating a meal of fried chicken tenders, cornbread, and macaroni and cheese, such a turn that night seemed remote. Between bites, Mom told stories in chains that in those minutes made me believe that she might just get up from her hospital bed and live on for weeks or months.

Though maybe she sensed something else.

To keep her talking and to distract us from the end, my daughters requested that Mom help them order their lives. My older daughter Pari urged her to draw a landscape design for Pari's home in Hot Springs, Virginia. We have that sketch, full of the various plants that would border and complement the house, with instructions on when to plant, when to dig up, and when to fertilize. My younger daughter Layla was more interested in recipes to carry on: frozen strawberry salad, chicken pot pie, and Mom's macaroni and cheese that somehow I could never duplicate well enough.

Home design and cooking were certainly two of Mom's strengths. As a little boy, I ran afoul of the neatness and order of her house, but I put myself in the kitchen every night to learn how to cook like she did—which ingredients to use, which brands, and how to coordinate the meal so that everything appeared on the table at the same time, all hot and fresh. This food was so delicious that it would make you drop to your knees and wonder why you ever asked for salad dressing on the side, a "vegetable medley" instead of scalloped potatoes, any pot of greens not cooked with side-meat, and tofu, quinoa, or "vegan cheese" as a substitute for anything.

Once I brought some friends home to spend the night. The next day we would be heading for a New Orleans food frenzy. That night at supper I kept bringing up all that good restaurant food we'd soon be sharing, and one of my friends, over a seven-layer salad and shrimp creole, looked at me in disbelief,

"How could it ever beat the food we're having here in 'this restaurant?'"

I felt like such a fool.

I know now that raw and undercooked vegetables are better for me, but please, season and cook my peas and beans and collard greens to death. And don't spare the pork. You can bet I won't.

I'm going on about food instead of telling the story I'm bound to tell, but a good food digression is in perfect keeping with everything my mother was, believed, and did when she told all those stories of her life.

So though I don't know the prompt for her next words, I do know it found its motivation somewhere and somehow in these supper moments.

Amidst our clamor, she cleared her voice, then announced to everyone, even the nurse who had stopped in to see if Mom wanted a Coke:

"Now y'all listen to me..."

We looked at her, all forgetting to breathe out.

"Now when I die..."

I can't begin to write the rush of fears and expectations of what I thought might follow. She and I had briefly discussed her funeral that morning. To indirectly get to the service I never wanted to plan, I asked about a good friend who passed the previous year and what music that woman had requested for her service.

"She chose 'When the Saints Go Marching In.' It's a good song, but I don't want anything like that at my funeral!"

"Well, what would you like?"

She thought a moment.

"That Beatles' song, '*Imagine*.'"

I didn't correct her--"Now Mom, John Lennon did that one"--mainly because I had no idea she loved this song and wanted it to send her off from this world, especially with that opening line. As far as I knew, Mom believed in heaven, and certainly her fellow Methodist church members did. I thought she might have chosen Willie Nelson's "Angel Flying Too Close to the Ground."

"And I want Sally Vines to play it on her saxophone."

At least the instrumental would keep the peace, especially coming from Sally, who was not only a professional musician, but also the daughter of the man Mom kept company with for fifteen years after my father passed. John Vines, another good man who, like my Dad, loved Mom's cooking and, of course, her.

"So, when I die, I want you to promise me something.

"Yes ma'am," Pari and Layla answered as one. "Whatever you want, Granma!"

I kept holding my breath, and oddly, I'm doing so now as I write these words. Would she want us to take her body "home," to Courtland, Alabama, where all her father's family, the Terry's, were buried? Did she want to be buried in a certain dress? Did she want us to care for her Maine Coon cat, Pepper?

Did she want us to ban any strange, unsavory relative from her funeral?

Before Mom's mother, my Nanny Ellen, died, she made us promise that under no circumstances were we ever to open the door should a "greasy fat man come walking up to the house."

"Who would that be, Nanny?" I asked.

"Iron Terry."

"Iron" Terry was Nanny's husband's half-brother. I never knew my grandfather nor had I ever seen most of his Courtland brethren, including the man whose name was actually "Arn."

While I promised Nanny that I would honor this wish, I wondered whether I would be able to pick out this greasy fat man if it ever came to it. After all, as I mentally scanned my neighborhood, my church, and the community of Bessemer itself, I figured that I had just promised to keep out three-quarters of the older men who might want to respect Nanny at her end. And even if I did manage to sense Iron's coming, could a fifteen year-old boy like me really deny entrance to an elder, a relative to boot?

Of course, on the day after she died, among the well-wishers was a smiling man who entered our dining room before I had a chance to do anything except shake his hand. I don't know if he just walked in, as many were doing, or if he rang the bell and was ushered in by my well-meaning father.

"Hey Buddy, I'm your Uncle Arn."

Internally I screamed; externally I said "Nice to meet you." I thought of Nanny, and though I didn't understand it then, I accepted later that in times of death, grief, and mourning, not all promises make it past the proprietary gatekeeper.

Maybe he drank too much, and maybe he cheated somebody out of something. I was never sure of Nanny's grudge against him, but on this day, as we broke a near deathbed promise, all I saw was a nice man who offered me his sorrow, smiling all the while.

Ol' Iron.

No one has issued me a deathbed wish since, as if they knew how unreliable I was. Yet, forty-seven years to the month after Nanny passed, here we were, waiting for what was to come.

"Now when I die, I want y'all to promise me that the first thing you'll do [before we cry and hug each other and close your eyes?] is to go into my bedroom, open up my top drawer, and throw away all my underwear."

She looked at us then, every one of us, in the eye, as she always did when uttering a pronouncement that we better not brook.

"That's right. I don't want anyone else touching it."

And it wasn't that we didn't take her seriously. It wasn't that we didn't understand that from a southern woman--one who insisted that every knife go on the right of the plate, and every fork on the left where it rested on top of the napkin; or that every bed in the house must be made by 9:00 in the morning; and that the house must be vacuumed four times a week regardless of whether only one person was still living there--this new declaration wasn't serious.

Oh, we knew.

Knowing, though, doesn't always reflect emotion, and the emotion we all felt was something between relief and hilarity. So we laughed, every one of us, a reaction that made Mom even more emphatic.

"I mean it now! All my underwear, just throw it away."

"Yes ma'am Granma!"

"Of course we will Jo Ann!"

"Yes, I'll take care of it, Mom."

"Well okay then," she said.

∫

"On Sunday morning a week later, Vivian lay awake in the bed watching the light fill the room and move up the dressing table, over the perfume bottles, across the chest of drawers, where Nebraska had, as always, neatly balled up and stored Edward's socks. Was there ever a time when it did not feel natural to have some other woman's hands fixing those socks?" (Hoffman, *Almost Family*, 112)

As acts of intimacy go, taking care of someone's underwear, even someone's socks, ranks in the top five things we want only certain people to do.

When I think of my own underwear, I realize that only the following people have ever touched them:

My mother. My wife. My childhood family maid, Dissie Shepherd. Possibly my Nanny.

I guess it's not a surprising list, and most people's would be similar, in number anyway. My daughters have never laid a finger on my underwear, though they have no doubt handled their mother's, since in their teenage years when it was my turn to do the laundry, I often placed the wrong underwear in the respective dresser drawers. I'd see them marching into our bedroom with bottoms that they, at least, thought only an idiot would think were theirs. My wife would laugh, wondering how I could make such a mistake. But I ask you, what father knows or should know exactly whose female underwear is whose?

I hope my daughters will be spared from having to deal with my underwear. Some things should be kept from children even when they're adults for as long as possible. Not that there weren't occasions when I retrieved my mother's and my underwear from her dryer. I'd fold each and carefully place hers on her bed, figuring that she could take care of placing them neatly in her bureau drawer. She'd thank me sometimes, or just as likely tell me that I didn't have to do *that*, *that* being as close as she'd come to referring to her bras and pants. I didn't know at the time what she thought about my handling her underthings, or if she thought about it at all.

I think I know now.

And even now when my wife and I fold clothes together, I want to snatch out of her hand every pair of boxers she takes up.

"Let me do that," as if folding my underwear were too ugly or crude for her; as if I'm sparing her from something she shouldn't have to do. As if she's never touched them otherwise.

She doesn't mind my folding hers, though she asks that I just place them on top of the dresser since I don't have the knack for putting anything neatly into a drawer.

My wife even selects and buys my underwear, somehow unwilling to leave me to my own devices in this area. I, of course, have only dreamed of buying hers. Still, I know we'll wash and fold each other's till the end.

I remember laughing when my mother told me the reason that she never planned to remarry after my Dad died:

"I just don't want to have to wash some old man's dirty underwear again!"

It's amusing the steps we take and the ones we don't as we move in and out of intimacy and ingrained pride.

I think of the "Grandmother" in Flannery O'Connor's "A Good Man Is Hard to Find," who dresses as if she's going to a luncheon at The Club when embarking with her family on a car vacation to Florida. She calculates that being dressed so primly and properly will allow anyone who finds her body on the side of the road, subsequent to the accident that she doesn't know she's foreshadowing, to see that she was "a lady." No doubt her old woman's underwear was pristinely chosen, starched, and pressed, too.

Or consider Alfred Uhry's *Driving Miss Daisy*. Though underwear is never seen nor remarked on, another act of intimacy forces us, if not the characters, to consider subtle southern ironies. After Daisy's maid/cook Idella has passed, Daisy takes to the kitchen to follow Idella's recipe for nurturing fried chicken. Her chauffer/caretaker Hoke enters the kitchen as Daisy shifts the drumsticks and thighs around the heated pan.

A white woman in the 1960's frying chicken, preparing a loving meal, for a black man roughly her age. For their supper.

It's an act of intimacy all right, though social codes and barriers cause them to take their plates and sup in adjoining rooms—Daisy in the formal dining room, Hoke at the kitchen table. They can *hear* each other chewing, though the *sight* of each other enjoying this meal remains forbidden. Maybe the scene is heavy-handed, but that doesn't mean it isn't true.

Toward the film's end, the desire for intimacy causes Daisy to proclaim that Hoke is "her best friend." I don't know if the filmmakers thought we couldn't handle an articulate response from Hoke, or if a man of this era answered in the way Hoke does because of those same social codes, but all he says in response is "Yassum." And when in the film's final scene in the nursing home, after Daisy shoos her son Booly away, Hoke lifts Daisy's fork and feeds this dying woman her Thanksgiving pecan pie, their intimacy, if not their deep friendship, forever sealed.

For years after my father died, my mother employed a man named Robert to help her in the garden, to clean her gutters, and do any other manual jobs her body and dignity wouldn't allow her to perform. She told me often of how she'd have to pick Robert up from his government-subsidized apartment, which a friend had pulled strings to get him into. Mom told me that Robert had been a policeman in Washington, DC, once, though what caused him to return almost penniless to Bessemer, where he was born, she never knew.

"He's really smart," she'd say, "and likes to read.

They discussed politics often and both lamented the decline in Bessemer's standards of formal education. On warm days Robert rode his bicycle to work, but as he aged, those good days dwindled. Some days he wouldn't show up at all, but Mom kept hoping that she could provide work and some income for him.

On the days Robert did come, she'd prepare his lunch, making him the fried bologna or tuna fish sandwiches she made for my brother and me when we were kids. She'd serve him on her everyday china, carrying his plate and glass of iced tea outside where he'd sit at the patio table and eat while she sat at her own kitchen table. Robert was ten years younger than Mom and always a gentleman, she said. A good companion.

Old times, though, aren't easily forgotten. My mother and grandmother always fed the hired help, white or black. Yet none of these men was ever invited to sit at the table with the family.

It's funny, but my mother also told me how particular Robert was about his meals, and she'd make special trips to the grocery store to buy what he liked on the days he worked. That seems like something intimate to me.

She also asked Robert to help her change the sheets on my bed just before my visits. That bed was antique, the mattress tight fitting, and it hurt her back to wrestle with it. I could have made my own bed when I arrived, but that isn't how my mother worked. I had to drive such a long way, and everything had to be just right for my arrival. She'd have a pot roast ready, with potatoes and carrots simmering next to the meat. The two of us would eat together, and later that night I'd rest in a bed that a grown man had made up for me. A man older than me. A black man, and despite all I want to believe, I cannot imagine my mother ever hiring a white man to do the same. In her last year of life, she hired a married couple to help her around the house, vacuuming, dusting, and making up my old bed. They, too, were black.

I don't know if this couple helped Mom with her own bed, but I know Robert never did. This isn't something my mother told me; it's just something that I know from understanding all that was and wasn't allowed in our world.

I also know that as with my childhood maid Dissie, Robert had full bathroom privileges. I feel funny writing this, but my discomfort doesn't make it less true.

Maybe these aren't startling revelations. Yet as I consider the way we lived and interacted, I understand that there was always a greater intimacy than we acknowledged, or approved publicly. Others have written more eloquently and even academically about this truth. Sometimes, though, the only way to experience a political epiphany is to realize its personal origin.

§

Often, Dissie brought her granddaughter Juanita ('Nita) to play with my brother and me. We were kids reaching for adolescence, playing whiffle ball or other games appropriate to summertime Alabama, though we always played them in the back yard.

The way our house was structured, everyone passed through the bedroom my brother and I shared on the way from one end of the house to the other. Once, as I was changing clothes, Nita passed through. I was sitting in front of my dresser in my underwear, a pair of briefs. I suppose I couldn't decide which pair of play-shorts to wear, but what I remember most is that when I heard her coming, I knew I couldn't hide or scramble fast enough to put those covering pants on. And for some reason, my throat sealed up, too, so when Nita passed, I just sat there with a stupid smile on my face.

She smiled, too, and maybe she said "Sorry Buddy," but neither of us spoke of that moment again.

Juanita, then, was the only girl to see me in my underwear until college, until a girl named Lisa. Something is always beyond our control: moments of intimacy that we don't plan on but can't forget.

So what I'm saying is that laws and society and social custom attempting to guard our blood purity and intimate feelings are pure bullshit. What we end up "protecting" and countenancing is never what we intend.

Or pretend.

§

My mother died late on a summer Saturday night. My brother Mike, Sallie Vines, and my wife and I were gathered round her. My wife spoke words of love to help her pass. And then we began to mourn with Mom's community.

> "Neighbors bring food with death and flowers with sickness and little things in between. Boo was our neighbor. He gave us soap dolls, a broken watch and chain, a pair of good-luck pennies, and our lives. But neighbors give in return. We never put back into the tree what we took out of it: we had given him nothing, and it made me sad' (TKAM 321).

Aside from believing that "Scout Finch" is wrong—surely she, "Jem" and "Dill" gave Boo Radley pleasure as he watched them and saw the picture of what a relatively happy childhood was like—I love the acknowledgment in that passage of all that neighbors do to comfort and support and abide with us through our intimate sorrows.

My mother's community fed us well in the week before and after she passed. Friends kept calling and dropping by to see her through the day that she died, and up until her last hours, my mother continued to regale her friends with the personal stories that she always loved to tell of her past and their adventures together.

I continue to see images of this community over those last hours: my oldest friend Freddy sitting by my mother's hospital bed, holding her hand, something he never did before, though as his mother did with me, Mom embraced Freddy when we were boys, and surely changed his pants when it was called for; Mom's next door neighbor, Helen, and her sisters coming over and praying with Mom, and then frying catfish for us on the night before Mom passed; Mom's best friend Jane Mulkin sitting on the floor by her recliner where Mom spent the last thirty-six hours of her life. I didn't listen to everything they said in those hours, but Jane told me later that Mom had asked her how long she thought Mom had left, something neither Jane nor anyone else could tell her.

Something my mother chose not to ask my brother or me.

The last food my mother ate with anything like enjoyment was a ramekin of baked vanilla custard Jane made for her. I sat by her as she spooned every bit of that custard herself. My mother never let nor needed me to feed her.

Had we not been there, had there been no one else, Mom would have asked Jane to throw out her underwear, something Jane would have gladly done. She asked me after Mom passed if we had done as instructed.

"Yes," I said. "Of course. It was the first thing I did the next morning."

An independent woman always, her final request, then, can be seen as amusing, predictable, appropriate, and even homage to old-time Southern propriety and decorum.

Yes, but it was also an intimacy she conferred on us. A last chore with which she graced us. It is only in such intimacies that we can truly measure the depth of our love and trust in each other.

An original concession to the inevitable.

A way of saying, "I'm yours."

# As I Lay Dreaming of S-Town

"...and us setting in the house in the winter, listening to it, [and]
I would think what a shame Darl couldn't be to enjoy it too. But
it is better so for him. This world is not his world; this life his
life" (261).

It was in graduate school that I first read Faulkner's minor
masterpiece, *As I Lay Dying*. As in much of Faulkner, I didn't understand
exactly what the lines above meant, what exactly "Cash" meant about his
younger brother "Darl." In fact, I wasn't sure about most of the novel; I
understood what happened, but I didn't approach it or retreat from it with
the same somberness and gravity that I did with *Absalom, Absalom!, The
Sound and the Fury*, or *Light in August*. So much of the Bundren family and
their journey to bury "Addie," their wife/mother, fell from my head. Except
these lines, and though I couldn't quite figure out their literal or emotive
meaning, I kept hearing their haunting echo.

It's been almost forty years since that first reading, and I've read
and taught the novel many times since. I am not a Faulkner scholar, but I
do understand what Cash is saying to Darl now, and that understanding is
focused on what it means to be a Southern misfit, especially within your
own family.

At the novel's end, the Bundrens decide they must commit Darl
to the asylum in Jackson, or else the constable will arrest him for burning
a barn, lock him in a cell somewhere for good, and, more importantly
perhaps, force the Bundrens to pay for all damages. Cash convinces his
brother that this course is best, though only after his other brother and
sister, Jewel and Dewey Dell, and their father, Anse, jump on Darl, hold
him down, and then shut him up in the wagon that will transport him to
his new forever home.

Sure, Darl has strangely prophetic visions, and he torments Jewel,
his half-brother, mercilessly with the circumstances of Jewel's engendering.

Yes, he burns down a neighbor's barn, mainly because his mother's odorous and rotting corpse outrages him. He's a strange one, especially to the other Bundrens.

A family misfit.

He's dangerous, too, because God knows what else he'd do if he wasn't bound for Jackson. His maniacal laughter ends his farewell section—a most disquieting end, and one that has staying power for most readers, and certainly for me.

Maybe within my memory I've always understood Darl, but as I listened and re-listened to *Serial* and *This American Life's* podcast, *S-Town*— the story of rural horologist John B. McLemore--my understanding of Darl, and Cash's words about him, have carbonized.

The mystery of John B. McLemore is not the mystery we encounter as the podcast begins. Through the work's seven chapters, we go inside Bibb County, Alabama, inside John, his family, those he hangs with, those he maybe loves, and certainly those he hates. By the end, and certainly in the trial that is proceeding in the series' aftermath, those John loved and those he hated might be one and the same.

Read the *S-Town* discussion page on Facebook, and you'll see that John's tormentors—his vultures and scavengers—are legion, with none of them agreeing on the villain's identity. Everyone in Bibb County, it seems, wants to find John B's "buried gold;" everyone has wondered how much he was truly worth. His surviving relatives and friends, like Tyler Goodson, believe they have rights to his property, that John B. meant to will them his left-behind goods and dogs, if only he had taken the time to draw up that will before he "transitioned."

The *Tuscaloosa* (Alabama) *News*, which I read daily online, featured a story recently about Tyler Goodson and his impending October trial for stealing John's property. Tyler denies the charge because he claims to know what John B meant him to have. The writer and narrator of *S-Town*, Brian Reed, might have to testify at the trial because *S-Town* uncovered certain evidence that could possibly determine the outcome of Tyler's trial.

Though I don't know any of these characters, I feel invested in their story. I do tangentially know Tyler Goodson's lawyer, JD Terry, the son of my childhood neighbor in Bessemer, a town mentioned in *S-Town* near Bibb County, and where Reed stays in the Best Western motel. More crucially for me, Chapter Two of the podcast features Tyler Goodson's tattoo parlor deep in the heart of my hometown. It is this setting, this place of business, that reveals the sort of misfit John B is and links him to Faulkner's Darl: men with visions; men who are tolerated and liked some of the time, but who are too different to be accepted by those they sometimes choose to, sometimes *must,* hang around.

Listening again to Chapter Two of *S-Town* unsettles me. One of the only places away from his home that John B visited was that tattoo parlor. Although John B hated tattoos and rednecks and drug users, he loved Tyler, and he felt accepted by the hangers-on there. The shop itself included the parlor in front, and, through a secret door, a bar that included a stripper's pole. Brian Reed also entered this world and heard things that made his hair and soul curl.

Of course, before his work on this story, Reed had never been to Bessemer. He's half-Jewish (full disclosure, as I am). And he's married to an African-American woman (full disclosure, my wife is Persian). And what he heard in Tyler's shop shook him. Yet, he escaped.

He could escape.

No one ganged up on Brian, and no one really ganged up on John B either. Everybody knew, however, just how different John B was from them: that he was highly educated, unlike them. That he no longer hated African-Americans, unlike them.

That he was gay, unlike them.

When John B finally left Bibb County, and this world, no one had jumped on him to do so. Instead, he left because he understood just how different he was from his Bibb County Shit-Town fellow citizens. From his family. He kept asking Reed, and surely himself, why he chose to stay in Woodstock, Bibb County, Alabama, for as long as he did. That he didn't leave sooner makes me thankful but also makes me wonder.

I am thankful that I did leave, though I go back several times a year to see my mother and friends.

But I wonder not only about John B's life, but about the other John B's I knew: older men I've judged, younger men I've counseled. Schoolmates I've ditched.

I am now understanding things about them that eluded me the first time through, just as I wondered about Darl after reading *As I Lay Dying* that first time.

Things about misfits, what makes them so, and how I respond to them, these people who have suffered and been ganged up on. Who have left this world, or maybe wish they had.

§

This world is not his world.

Since I teach at a small liberal arts college, I am freshman advisor to many kinds of students, not all of whom want to major in English. Most, though, do have a sense of who they are and who they want to be. On occasion, they want my input. "Help me decide whether to take Biology or Chemistry." "What could I do if I major in English?" Only rarely do I get one who has tested very highly on the placement exam but has "other issues."

Like Michael.

Extremely quiet, awkward, Michael was sitting very still on that first day in my office with his mother and stepfather. The parents asked questions about credit hours, meal plans, dorm life.

Michael said nothing.

In those days freshmen would arrive and check-in on a Friday and then have the entire weekend for orientation, outdoor "team-building" activities, street parties, and even church. Michael actually lived in the tiny town where our college was nestled. Late that afternoon, after his parents had returned home, Michael reappeared in my office. He stood just inside the door, shifting his feet, mumbling something I couldn't get.

Michael had soft blond hair, wore thick glasses, and didn't quite fit his baggy jeans. He was trying for long sideburns and a goatee, but his facial hair still had that downy fuzz that marks a guy who hasn't begun shaving and might never need to.

"Michael," I asked, "is something wrong?"

He wouldn't look at me and kept shifting his oversized white Reeboks.

Finally he looked up and almost whispered,

"I'm homesick."

I understood. I remembered.

When my own parents dropped me off at college and then drove the 25 miles back to our house, I felt that stomachache that periodically plagued me all the way back to kindergarten, perhaps even earlier when I'd be sent to play at another kid's house. At college, though, I knew my roommate, and at supper that first night I met others and soon was attending organizational meetings at the newspaper and entertainment committee offices.

I was able to adjust to new situations.

I could sense Michael wasn't.

"Well, you don't absolutely need to be here, Michael. Where does your family live?"

"Oh, just about a mile away."

"Well then if you're having a hard time, just go on home. We won't be registering for classes until Monday."

He half-smiled and said, "Thank you sir." I thought about Michael over that weekend, and the dread, I'm sure, he was feeling when Sunday night came upon him.

I wondered then and still do now whether or not I did the right thing by him.

In spite of everything, he lasted; he remained my advisee, declaring his English major when he was a sophomore. Almost four years later, on the verge of graduating, Michael dropped by my office again.

"Sir, the registrar says I need one more science class to graduate."

I didn't believe this could be true. I am usually OCD about students' records and ensuring that they have taken their core courses. True enough, though, after checking Michael's online file, I found that he was short a science credit. Three hours short, which meant he'd have to enroll in summer school, and his straitened family would have to choke up additional funds.

And, that someone would have to break this news to his anxious mother.

On the following day Michael was scheduled to present his senior thesis, which his proud parents would attend.

"Will you help me tell them?" he asked.

It was the last thing I wanted to do, but it was also partly my fault, and wholly my responsibility.

"Yes, Michael, I will."

Though he struggled through his thesis because, obviously, public speaking was not Michael's strong suit, he made it and passed his seminar. After the presentation, I followed Michael and his clearly relieved mother out into the rotunda of our class building. Michael kept trying to slow his mother down, but she seemed to sense that the sooner she got out of there the better, as if someone might rush her and tell her that this was all an illusion—that something was wrong with this day, this time, this world of Michael.

Of course, something was:

"Mrs _____, I'm sorry to have to tell you this, but Michael and I made a mistake in keeping up with his credits. He's going to need to pass one more science class to graduate."

I had never seen a person literally sink before. But she caught herself before she hit: "Well...what does he have to do?"

I told her. I assured her that he would be able to walk at graduation, and after he passed the summer school class, the college would mail his diploma to him.

She sighed and looked to the ceiling as if somehow she had known this would happen.

"Well, all right...Come on Michael."

Michael looked back at me then:

"Thank you, sir."

Michael passed his science class, and then he graduated. That was six years ago, when he walked out of the college and into—or perhaps out of—this world.

I don't know what happened to him afterward. One of my colleagues who remembers him well recently told me that once, during those years, Michael came to him, threatening suicide. At least he asked for help, then. And now?

I keep telling myself, his life is not my life.

§

In my life in Bessemer—so close to John B's "shit-town" of Woodstock that I could drive there sooner than I could listen to an entire episode of the podcast--I could have applied Cash Bundren's words about brother Darl to quite a few people I knew. I could even say that like Dewey Dell and Jewel, and like the men at Tyler Goodson's tattoo parlor, Black Sheep Ink, I at least thought about and sometimes did jump on some of these characters.

In Chapter Two, Brian speaks at length with the guys at Black Sheep Ink about John B, out of John B's presence. They have been discussing John B's penchant for launching into "tirades" about how they're all "failures;" about how they'll "never amount to nothing;" about how they don't understand or care about realities like climate change and our over-consumption of fossil-fuels. While they might eye-roll John B or smile at each other as he rants,

"These guys dish it out, too. They tease John for his many peculiarities, like how he'll devour whatever leftover food is around, no matter how old or rock-hard it is, his inability to buy new shoes to alleviate his athlete's foot, which he's allegedly had for three years, his extemporaneous solving of math problems, his utter aversion to being in a room with more than two or three people at a time, his living with his mom his whole life, his being a loner. It's friendly, though. They like John. After all, John is the granddaddy of all black sheep, so this crew gets him. They truly seem to accept him, though that doesn't stop them from wonderin'."

So much to wonder about John B: his money, his "lifestyle," why he wants to hang around them when he hates so much about them, especially their racism and their tattoos. Tyler Goodson will later tell Brian Reed that he loves John B, that whenever he leaves John B's house, they both say, "I love you man." Tyler understands that John B's orientation might be way different than his own, but he says that his friend has never tried anything with him.

I keep seeing scenes of this tattoo parlor, of John B's haranguing the assembled others who are so unlike him. Of their joking with him, accepting him in a certain way, but never fully. I believe that if it came down to it, they would use him, hurt him, gang up on him for his money and his property. Though they are all black sheep—as is the entire Bundren family—John B is a misfit too far.

As I might say about Lewis Mincey, a kid I knew in Bessemer. A kid who so closely resembled *A Confederacy of Dunces'* main character, Ignatius J. Reilly, that when I first read that novel in grad school, I thought my life was being self-reflected:

"Shifting from one hip to the other in his lumbering, elephantine fashion, Ignatius sent waves of flesh rippling beneath the tweed and flannel, waves That broke upon button and seams...It seemed as if his whole being was Ready to burst from his swollen suede desert boots" (1-2).

Lewis Mincey described to a tee.

"Elephantine," over six feet tall in high school, weighing, I'm guessing, close to 275 (not a one of them muscle pounds), with knees that touched at the cap, and feet almost at right angles from each other. These attributes helped him in one way:

His ability to spell out words with his body.

In tenth grade English class, in our afternoon Thespian Club meetings and play rehearsals, our teacher often called on Lewis to spell things, and Lewis, of course, didn't exactly need the prompting. I can see him now, contorting:

"This is my 'Y,' this is my 'P.' Now my 'Q' needs work."

His classmates encouraged him, if "encouraged" is the right word. Egged him on? Provoked him? Asked for him to provide that day's entertainment, something we could rehash later that night as we phoned ourselves into delirium.

And delirium is right.

In my junior year of high school, the Thespian Club went to our regional convention in Birmingham, where my friends Jimbo and Mary Jane, and I performed a one-act play for competition. Some of our other friends, our "stage crew," went, too, and these guys, along with our advisor, got hotel rooms. The cast went back to our family homes after that first night of the convention because our performance came early the next morning, and the last thing we needed was to stay out most of the night getting shit-faced drunk, as our crew did.

I pick the phrase "shit-faced" carefully. I think hearing it, we all get a certain image of a goofy grin, slobber dripping from a drunken mouth, eyes crossed or nearly there.

What most of us don't, won't, can't, imagine is what the crew reported to us the next day. Lewis was one of this crew, and given his stature and girth, he could knock back plenty of beer and whiskey, which he did that night.

How do we measure phrases and degrees of "holding one's liquor?"

For Lewis, the other crew members didn't measure in the usual form, the degree of hurling that so many of us achieve when we've imbibed too heavily. No, they used another yardstick:

"We lost him at some point," they said, "and when we got back to the room, he was passed out in his own shit."

Apparently, it was everywhere: the bed, the carpet, all over the bathroom.

It's crude of me to report this, I know. I do so, however, because like those who actually saw it, I went back to school the next week and reported on the scene of Lewis's defecating humiliation far and wide. Lewis never had a chance after that night, if he ever did before. Still, he finished high school, was even the co-star of his senior play, Aristophenes' *The Birds*.

I had graduated the previous year but came back to see those of my friends who were still performing.

Was Lewis my friend? Did he consider himself to be my or anyone else's friend, or was he just a kid who never fit with us, or with himself?

He was actually quite funny in his own way, and no doubt brighter than most in our school. I lost track of him after that play, and it seems to me that a number of years back, I heard he committed suicide. I am not being intentionally vague about Lewis's end; I really don't remember the details, and so far, no one I knew back then remembers either, which is about as sad a testament to Lewis as I can say.

I knew Lewis early on. When we were little boys, I know we travelled the same kid birthday party circuits. My mother has recorded in my "Baby Book" a party at a friend's house, and among the "guests," (we were all two or three years old) is Lewis Mincey.

I do remember one other scene, though.

When I was seven, my grandmother, who lived with us, staged one of her notorious ladies' bridge parties on a night my parents had gone to the movies. She invited Lewis's grandmother who lived on the next block over from us. She was babysitting Lewis, so she brought him over to play with me. What we did together I can't remember, but at 8:30, I had to go to bed as no way would my parents or grandmother allow me to stay up one minute past my bedtime. The card party raged on, however, and ol' Lewis had to figure out some strategy for survival.

In that drifty period before I fell sleep, however, I heard him. I wasn't allowed to shut my bedroom doors, which accessed both my parents' bedroom and the hallway leading to our breakfast room. When I heard what I heard, I sat up. There was Lewis, standing by my bed staring at me, and before I could register what he was doing or intended on doing, his grandmother called for him.

Then, my grandmother shut my doors and I fell asleep, thinking of Lewis.

§

This life is not his life.

I've heard that sometimes people feel as if they are being guided by some external presence; that they are outside themselves, looking down on the awful thing that is happening in their conscious life.

When John B first contacted Brian Reed, how much of his story did he truly want to share? Was he crying out for help in figuring out who this man he had been watching his entire life, this John B McLemore, was?

Even with seven chapter-hours of *S-Town*, there is so much we will never know about John B and what made him the man he was.

The key could be such a small one, too, something he never told or something that happened when he was young and vulnerable. When he was unprotected.

Something like this.

I once knew a man, knew him when I was a boy and teenager. I worked for him one summer in his yard. I cut his grass, helped him lay gravel for his garden walkway and then pour cement into that same path. I weeded his flowers in the July Alabama sun, and for my trouble, he gave me three things:

Fifty cents an hour.

A slur at my father, a reaction to my dad's saying you shouldn't cut the grass too low or else the sun would dry it out and kill it:

"What your father knows about cutting grass is less than the amount of shit a Chihuahua makes."

And this scene.

I have finished cutting the grass, and he has arrived from his professional job. He wants me to help him lift some heavy rocks for the garden. He asks me to come inside while he changes. He must have asked me to follow him upstairs where he will change, because on my own I wouldn't have gone there, wouldn't have ascended his stairs. I am standing in the hallway leading to his bedroom. He does not shut his bedroom door, does not hide taking off his street clothes, does not cover or move out of sight as he reveals his gold underpants. Briefs, they were, much like the ones I was wearing underneath my jeans, only mine were plain white.

He doesn't look at me as he changes, though I turn quickly, so how can I be certain that he didn't?

He says nothing and soon has slipped into a gold work-suit, one-piece coveralls meant for cultivating.

It's like I was and wasn't there.

What if we had made eye contact? What else might he have done or said? As in dreams when we are caught by someone, or when someone is approaching us meaning to do us some harm, I see myself frozen in this moment.

We went downstairs then and out to the garden and lifted those heavy stones.

He lived alone with his mother. He was a man in his forties then, a man well-respected, though considered eccentric, even odd, by some. I was fifteen. In his spare time, he painted in pastels and watercolors. I have one of his pieces, a work given to me by my mother.

He never touched me, but I believe he wanted to.

Nothing like this ever happened again.

Through years of therapy, I know how possible it is to have scars even when you haven't been touched.

I can't help wondering, though: what if I hadn't resisted his overture, his grooming? What if he had beckoned me into his room? Would I have obeyed? Would I have fled? Or would I have remained still, rooted to that spot?

Paralyzed?

What if I hadn't been stronger, hadn't sensed the danger?

Hadn't escaped my S-Town?

∫

I know that many of us both love and hate our homes, our past. Despite my difficult experiences growing up in Bessemer, I didn't really want to leave.

In fact, I feared entering any new space where I didn't know if I'd make it; if I'd be good or smart enough to make it.

So I chose a college only 25 miles from home. Even when I went to graduate school in Knoxville, TN, I came home every chance I got. At first.

I don't know what would have happened had I stayed in Bessemer. I'm not saying I would have ended up like the man I described above, or like Lewis Mincey, or John B. McLemore. They had their own private hells. And, I assume, I would have had mine.

If I had another family, John B's family, for example, I might have been allowed or even encouraged to wallow in my fear of leaving home. With a more limiting or needy family, I might have chosen to live in my parents' spare room or have decided to get a low-rent apartment in nearby Jonesboro. I might have taken unsatisfying work in my hometown and never realized my potential, never gained the independence I needed, and never found the happiness I know.

Without my own family's support and encouragement of the dreams I had, I might not ever have left home at all.

§

In the last chapter of *S-Town*, we discover that John B paid Tyler Goodson to tattoo him all over his torso, to pierce and re-pierce his nipples, and to whip him repeatedly and then cover the lash marks with more tattoos. John B desired the principle of pleasure/pain, but then, hadn't his whole life been lived on that spectrum?

We also learn, and here is a southerner's true lament, of John B's history with race, as Brian Reed narrates:

"John had a complicated and contradictory relationship to race. Like with women and gay people, he'd express outrage when he heard examples of discrimination. He'd express empathy, and also an understanding for the systemic ways our society is built, to be unfair and harmful to these groups of people.

But then sometimes John would say racist things in front of me. He'd acknowledge that he shouldn't use the n-word and then use the n-word. People who've known him for a long time have told me that, especially years ago, John was quite racist, but that over the years he had changed for the better. Granted, these are white people telling me this.

Woodstock is about 95% white, which, of course, is not an accident. It's the result of many decades of laws and violence and day-to-day racism. Bibb County was the last county in Alabama to comply with a school desegregation order in 1967, long after *Brown v. Board of Education*. It's a place that voted for George Wallace four to one. And then in the '50s, had a sign appear on Main Street in one of the towns saying, "The Klan people of Bibb County welcome you."

So much of the stuff John said he hated about Shittown—Harleys, tattoos, misogyny and homophobia, racism, he said he despised it. But that stuff was part of him, too."

My town, Bessemer, had a Klan welcome sign, too, back in the 1950's. Recently, I found a photo of it, planted there next to signs from the Kiwanis, Jaycees, and Lions. Unlike John B, I am not gay, but have been called "queer" or "fag" for simple things like growing my hair long, loving David Bowie, refusing to try out for football. No one ever ganged up on me or beat me, though. I've never used a racial slur publicly. Or at least not as an adult.

But I will admit that long ago, after my first daughter was born, my father said to me as we were out walking one spring afternoon,

"I'm afraid she'll grow up and marry someone black."

In that moment I was scared, too. I could feel his fear, and though it didn't totally become my own, it never left me.

And yet I know that, compared to all the others I've written about here, I have been inflicted with only a few, mostly hidden, scars from this world.

Hearing about John B, remembering Lewis and Michael, I realize I was strong. I am strong.

I escaped this world. My S-Town.

And entered the rest of my life.

# Goin' Up the Country

As we drive up the main street of town, I see three men sitting on their front porch, shirts off, their longish hair that indeterminate white-yellow color. They see me on the passenger's side, and they wave as if they know me, as if I'm a neighbor or family, and not the curious invader I am. For I am on their home ground, and my intentions aren't exactly noble, or even good.

No one else in the car notices them. Jimbo is driving, his partner Michael and my brother Mike in back. Michael's GPS tells us that we're right smack-dab in West Blocton, though it can't tell us where to go to find what we're really seeking.

I don't think this way when we pass them, but later, I wonder if those three men--who might be brothers or cousins or just old friends--aren't what I was supposed to find. I bet they never have to call each other to ask if they might drop by. I bet that one drifts over about 4:30 every day, the other following not long after, and they sit and drink Cokes or Milwaukee's Best until supper is ready.

Their image sticks with me, but it's not the only or even the main one on this day—a day when my grief hasn't fully hit me, but instead has set me adrift, left me untethered to anything I might call real, or even "home."

I've always assumed that people of my region and culture gather for supper every night about 6:00, because that's the story of my old friends and me. We had to be at our supper table by 6 or our mothers would be calling out in the yard for us and then on the phone to each other. Being late to my mother's supper table is what I've always pictured or known as having "hell to pay." I've never tasted food better than hers, and so for all of my life with her, I was rarely late. But my mother died four days ago, and in this car now, if we don't get a move on, I think we'll be late for supper at Jimbo's house. I feel an old anxiety rising even though Jimbo says not to worry, that it'll be fine. Still, because I know that there are fresh summer vegetables and a pan of cornbread waiting on us, I hear *my* mother's voice:

"Y'all better come on now. That supper will ruin."

We have other things to worry about, though, as we pass the town center. Michael's GPS isn't commenting on our path any longer because out here there is no service. We might not be lost on this semi-misguided trip, but we sure as hell can't be found.

And the road we're depending on vacated its center and side stripes a mile back.

∫

On the road trips my mother and I used to take, whether to Publix Market, to downtown Bessemer's finest restaurant—The Bright Star—or to my house back in South Carolina, Mom regularly pointed out the same houses or memory place-markers:

"There's Durwood's house," she'd say, or "There's the man with his little horses. They're so cute. You know he used to have Emu's?"

And on Interstate 20, near Carrollton, Georgia:

"There's the place where our car stalled that time we were coming back from visiting you. Your daddy and I had to stay at that Days Inn up there."

Back in Bessemer, she and I would pass rolling hills, pastures of grazing cows, and new subdivisions usually beyond the city limits so that those citizens wouldn't be bound by Bessemer taxes or city schools. She'd tell me what these developments used to be when she was a girl. There wasn't much for me to say, but after all, it was mainly my ear and my memory she was after.

I never once told her that I already knew Durwood's house, had been there with her, and had even gone to junior high with his daughter Janice. I honored her need to repeat these life signs, for this countryside was my mother's lifetime home. It wasn't all she knew but it was what she knew best.

It was what she loved more deeply than anything else.
She lamented her hometown's deterioration, the abandoned houses, especially the ones that had stood for nearly 100 years.

--"I wish somebody would just buy that house and fix it up. It's got history and would make such a nice home again."

On my next visit, as likely as not, the house would be a pile of rubble, wasted bricks wondering why they had been abandoned, or ever fired in the first place.

Bessemer similarly abandoned Arlington Elementary school, which my mother and I both attended. It stood for one hundred years, the last ten as a massive crack house. Arlington is a vacant lot now, not even a memory-marker.

My mother loved Bessemer despite its flaws, despite the carcass of its life lying before the world's eyes. She loved driving through town or the rural places on Bessemer's outskirts, soaking in the air as if she were ingesting something curative, palliative.

It's from her that I get so many of my habits, my love of reading and writing, and my yearning to drive the back roads near and around my home. Remembering, as if I might one day forget.

So yes, a road trip through the area always seems like a good idea to me, and usually, I don't care about establishing a destination, because I know that wherever I ride, I'll find the way back to where I started.

§

In the week after her death and before her funeral, my childhood friend Jimbo and his husband Michael came to Bessemer to help me grieve. My brother Mike and I met them at Jimbo's parents' house, just over the hill from where my mother lived. We had barely settled over cups of coffee when Jimbo suggested, with that familiar gleam in his eye that I recognized as the kind of trouble I wanted to dive into with him,

--"Let's take a road trip."

--"Where do you want to go?"

--"Let's see infamous Bessemer, and then let's go to 'S-Town!'"

"S-Town" is one of the most listened to podcasts in podcast history, produced by *Serial* and *This American Life*. Jimbo first alerted me to it, calling me one spring afternoon a year ago, "Buddy, drop whatever you're doing. You have to listen to this now!"

I was grading student essays, and needed no coercion. I'm not a great listener; my mind doesn't find easy resting places. So I was drifting at first even though I love a good murder mystery. Drifting until I heard,

--"The nearest city of any size is Bessemer..."

Then I was hooked, even though I knew that if my hometown were involved, the story would be grisly. And it was, especially if your bent is toward random and sketchy tattoo parlors, garden mazes, horology, and sadism, not exactly in that order and not exactly all in Bessemer.

"S-Town" is actually a community in neighboring Bibb County, which, heading southwest, a Bessemer citizen might reach within fifteen minutes. The question is, why would you want to reach it? More pointedly, why did Jimbo, or really any of us want to go there? Since the protagonist of the story, John B. McLemore, is dead, what on earth could we want there? What could we be seeking? Is wanting to go there like driving through the Midwest and wanting to stop in Holcomb, Kansas, just to see where the Clutter family lived? As if doing so might bring enlightenment rather than satisfying some prurient urge.

Exactly what is the matter with us for harboring such desires?

Bibb County holds such "towns" as West Blocton, Johns, Green Pond, and Caffee Junction. The most famous person to emerge from this locale was former New York Yankees announcer Mel Allen, aka Melvin Israel, which means, yes, there were once Jewish people in "S-Town."

The podcast also alerts us to the fact that the KKK has a strong presence in Bibb County and indeed used to have a "welcome" sign situated on the main county highway leading into West Blocton.

This news isn't exactly startling.

Brian Reed, who wrote and narrated the podcast, is half-Jewish. He got used to the area somehow, though I'm not sure he ever felt welcome or met another Jew. He had his staff with him, though, and I'm sure they had a GPS, but listening to the story's evolution, I don't see how extra company or navigation could be comforting or mooring to this outsider.

I had heard of this area best through my mother who, as an interior designer for a local Bessemer carpet and drapes retailer, used to travel through what we know as "S-Town," giving estimates, measuring houses and trailers for carpet and Astroturf, and hardly ever getting lost on her journey. She never admitted to feeling anxious about entering the houses down there, and she said that everyone treated her nice, though they often couldn't afford the new carpet they wanted.

--"Mainly," she'd report, "they just want some of that 'grass.' I feel sort of sorry for them," she'd go on, and yes, her sympathy was aroused in part by their poverty, but likely as not, more so by their "terrible taste."

I'd listen to her stories on the phone or when I returned to Bessemer from college and grad school. I considered her brave for taking on a career in mid-life and traveling to places that I surely wouldn't be comfortable entering. These weren't exactly "her people," but her parents had risen from rural people, and she still had many cousins who lived "out in the sticks." So she knew how to talk to these customers, and how to listen to them.

But she was always glad to be home again after encountering them.

How different can Bessemer people be from West Blocton people? Listen to "S-Town" and then we can talk.

While Bessemer is a real city with a population of 25,000-plus, Caffee Junction is just that, a crossroads where you can travel on to Tuscaloosa or to Green Pond. There's a gas station/convenience store at the junction and a barbecue joint. On our "S-Town" journey, even though the hickory smoke pit sorely tempted us, we were saving ourselves for supper. Anyway, my brother had carried a container of Joyce's cheese straws with us, just in case.

And if there is a pond in Green Pond, I've still never seen it. "Still," I say, because as we took off for our infamous Bessemer tour on this early August afternoon, and as we made it past and through the sites, our GPS didn't know how to lead us beside this particular still water, or to tell us if such a pond existed at all.

So if you choose to go looking, be warned.

∫

As I think back on all we saw and did that afternoon, the thing that surprises me most is that no music accompanied our trip. Maybe we needed the quiet background so that our voices were distinct, so that we might be better able to hear the nuances of pain, hilarity, questioning, and disagreement about all we saw and what it meant.

But I didn't think about this lack as we started out. I wanted to give my passengers a taste of Bessemer's darkness.

First, I directed Jimbo to drive up the Super Highway toward Birmingham.

--"Now, just as you pass over the bridge, take a right...that way."

We parked in front of a vacant lot, a place I had never noticed before reading about it.

--"This was the site of Lorene's Café, a Klan hangout. In fact, this is where the Bessemer Klansmen retreated after they killed Viola Liuzzo down in Selma during the March."

--"But this is near Daddy's store," Jimbo said, and indeed, the former site of Mulkin Auto Parts was only two blocks away. Not that the two were associated, but in Bessemer, you were never far enough away from someone or some thing that might get you into trouble, that might demonize your dreams.

--"And after they cooled off at Lorene's that night, one of them drove up 19<sup>th</sup> or 20<sup>th</sup> Street to Fairfax Avenue, turned left, and came to his own house six blocks later," I continued.

I discovered this fact doing my own research last year for an essay I wrote about Bessemer's Klan in the 1960's. Discovering this residence shocked me partly because the house was in a predominantly Black neighborhood, but more pointedly because those six blocks were the only buffer between this Klansman's house and my family's. I thought about taking us on this leg, but it was too out of the way and we had so much more to see.

And maybe because it pains me to see how rundown my old neighborhood has become.

We got back on the highway toward Birmingham, and as we rode under the first train trestle, I stopped us again.

--"Over to the right was Moose Park, where the Moose Lodge, formerly known as The Barn, was located."

This site, too, was vacant, weeds and Johnson grass owning it as if nothing had ever existed before them.

No one in Bessemer remembers that there was ever a Loyal Order of Moose, much less a lodge or park. The Barn had been a nightclub and perhaps a restaurant too, but this building and land are most infamously known for hosting a KKK rally back in 1963 that burned three crosses and stopped traffic up and down the highway. Charles Portis, later author of *True Grit*, reported the rally for *The New York Herald Tribune*; on this night, some of the assembled Klansmen later journeyed to Birmingham and bombed the AG Gaston Motel where Dr. King was staying. He wasn't in his room at that hour, though, and so escaped his fate for another few years.

--"Now just past this second train trestle is where the KKK had their welcome sign," an image I finally saw in Jonathan Bass's recent book, *He Calls Me By Lightning*, a story of another infamous Bessemer murder.

I don't know if it's possible to believe or disbelieve all that went on in our home town, but as we sat in the car gazing at a memory that wasn't exactly ours, I'm not sure why we thought it would be such fun to dredge up these particular horrors.

Is this what the nostalgia resulting from a loved one's death does to you: makes you want to see something worse than what you already feel? A pain akin, but also disassociated from that hole in your heart that you'll bear forever? Maybe, but I didn't have time for such reflection then.

--"Let's go on down to S-Town now,"

Michael implored, as if being there would provide some kind of answer.

∫

"Gonna leave the city, got to get away."

To get to Bibb County, one may choose the expedient way—down I-59—or the fun way, down 4th Avenue, the old Tuscaloosa Highway. The latter is the route my mother would have driven to Green Pond, and it was the choice my dad always made when he took me to football games at the University. In those times, I remember that for long stretches of road, the only sites would be cattle grazing or thick piney woods. Today, it's housing developments everywhere the eye can see.

"I don't even know this place," Jimbo shouted, and I wondered how many times someone like him had yelled about what we'd lost.

We passed Plantation Manor nursing home where my father's

mother spent her last days and where I once visited her brother Moe when he was so far gone.

The week before Mom died, when an officious hospice worker told us that in five days we'd have to move my mother either to a nursing home or back to her home, without care, my wife and daughters toured Plantation Manor.

"Just no," they said as one. "Granma can't go there. And we're glad you didn't come with us to see it."

They didn't explain their refusal, and as I found my memories, I knew they didn't have to.

We also passed a building that used to be a nursery where Mom bought more plants than any woman had need or right to buy. It was a pleasant garden owned by the niece of a girl I crushed on in eighth grade.

Now it's a Vape shop.

Our old friend Sarah's house came just after, on the right. We don't know what happened to her, and as we passed, I kept thinking of how each Sunday she and I would compare our respective Sunday lunches, who had the most vegetables, and which mayonnaise we'd use to relish our fresh tomatoes. Hers was Bama; mine Hellman's. We thought that these things mattered back then, and they did, because they're indicative of family folkways, and of what our mothers taught us. I'm sure Sarah's mother is gone, and I wonder if Sarah ever drives back here, to feel all she's missing, to see what's no longer there.

I wondered, too, what Jimbo was thinking now, if he was remembering what I did. He claims to have a poor memory, but I've learned that just a trigger is enough sometimes.

--"Your old girlfriend Theresa lived up there," I said as we passed yet another subdivision.

--"Yeah, and what about that girl who lured me to her house? She was older than us, and I didn't know any better than to go over there."

I thought for a minute.

--"Susie Allen?"

--"Yes!"

And then we cracked up, and I wondered what poor Michael thought about his husband, his past exploits. It can't be easy sitting in back when two old friends get going, when none of their memories seems particularly attractive or even enlightening.

--"So Michael," I said as I leaned back toward him, "here's a place you should know about. The Green Lantern."

How do I describe The Green Lantern? An off-white cement block building with a green roof that looks like it was built ninety years ago or last week?

--"Now, it's got a bit of history," I said, "though I hear it's cleaned itself up recently."

On a visit home a few years back, I read a story in *The Birmingham News* about the new owners of The Green Lantern and how they wanted to make the place a draw again for locals and for people from surrounding counties. You know, a place where you could get hamburger, shoot some pool, throw darts, have a beer or two. I thought plenty of times about trying it out because I like pool and Budweiser.

--"That is one place," Michael said, "that no one here is dragging my gay ass into."

--"We'll be with you Michael. What's to worry about?"

But as I thought about my pacifist bent, not to mention my arthritic hands, my brother's bad hip and shoulders, and Jimbo who, while once kicking a bullying galoot literally in the ass, had never to my knowledge been in any kind of fight, I wondered whether in the years since that article, the Lantern had reverted to its ignoble past.

--"Okay, well maybe not today," I said, and we cracked up again.

And then, we passed over the Bibb County line.

∫

--"Just exactly where I'm going, I cannot say."

Driving down Highway 11 toward Tuscaloosa I thought again of the days when my daddy took me to Alabama football games. On those Saturdays, the world consisted of Daddy, me, and a bunch of guys I didn't know wearing Crimson. I loved those games, but as funny as it sounds, I think I loved the rides down and back even more. I could sit in the front seat, and Daddy would describe all that we saw, the places he used to see every week from his bus seat as he traveled from his Birmingham home to college.

I never worried that we would get lost or stuck in a place where we weren't wanted or welcome. My daddy kept me anchored to him.

Now, as I think about my Jewish father taking his little boy through places that harbored both good and bad intentions—"home cooking," rambling shacks with outhouses so similar that it was hard to tell the one from the other, and trailers with rebel flags whose occupants might or might

not be related to the infamous KKK Imperial Wizard, Tuscaloosa's own
Bobby Shelton—I wonder if Dad was scared, intimidated, or even mildly
cautious about what would happen if our Pontiac or Buick were to stall. He
never acted worried, which meant I was free to love this experience: this
two-lane highway, my Dad, the game to come. And the ride home when
we'd listen to the post-game scoreboard.

Before hitting "S-Town," our crew traveled to the Mulkin's farm
somewhere out in the county. We inspected the formal gardens Jimbo's
mother Jane continuously updated and added to; we watched Jimbo's dad
Jim Ed catch another wide-mouth bass from a lake that I best remember as
hiding the first water moccasin I ever saw. A man killed that snake with an
old oar, and you know it takes a brave SOB to do that.

Jimbo, our friends, and I spent many nights at the farm when
we were college-aged. I never feared for my safety out here, so far away
from the life I knew. Anyone could have found us and done whatever they
wanted. But I guess that could happen in the city, too, at any time.

Soon, after fresh lemonade and more cheese straws, we got back in
Jimbo's rented hybrid and headed toward Bibb County.

Michael volunteered to direct us with his I-Phone. I say this as
much to add precision to the narrative as to show just how complacent we
were, we town boys who figured we were somehow insulated against self-
inflicted trouble.

--"Idiots,"

my mother might have said of us, even though most of these roads
are clearly marked and even though we are grown men. She would have
thought that the time for road trips begins early in the day, not when the
rural Alabama sun is within two hours of setting.

Michael got us on the county road toward West Blocton without too
much trouble. We passed lakes and nice houses displaying the American
flag. I don't own an American flag myself, but when I was a kid, I had a

Confederate flag pinned to my bedroom wall. It was three by five feet. I never asked for it and I don't know what eventually happened to it.

We passed occasional Alabama Crimson Tide flags, too, and if there any Auburn pennants down here, they're as carefully hidden as Obama signs.

Actually, there were no Trump signs either, a wonder in this reddest of states.

The two-lane road leading toward West Blocton—toward because we eventually had to take a left turn to get to "downtown" West Blocton—was pockmarked by two features.

First, the hilly roadside displayed mounds of Alabama's famous red dirt, which as a little boy, Mike called "meat." I don't know if he literally thought the red soil was meat, but I have to agree that when compared to the molded rising rump roasts Mom would buy for Sunday lunch, the two reds did resemble each other, the white fat on top of the meat resembling those washed-out weedy tops of the dirt mounds.

The other central feature was the automobile junkyards we kept passing. I can't say definitively how many there were, but when I started counting, I hit six in a two-mile distance. Is the number one activity/business/pastime of Bibb Countians to pass through mountainous legions of dead cars looking for alternators, carburetors, or precious gilded wheels? Another old friend of mine, Joe, tells me that "Yes, there's big money in old car parts."

If there had been people scouring those lots for anything, I'd understand the demand. But there was no sign in these weedy lots of anyone searching or doing anything at all, including whoever managed them.

This, too, was a sign of something, though as we drove further, I had no idea what, other than that Bessemer, with its abundance of auto parts dealers and "Cash for Gold" palaces, might not be the most desolate, hopeless, or peculiar place I know.

Despite the mystery, or because of it, I grew excited as we neared West Blocton. I love seeing small southern towns because they're full of history and you never know when or where you might find folk art, true antique furniture, former Jewish businesses or residents like Melvin Israel, or the best ribs you've ever eaten.

Or three bare-chested old men sitting on their front porch, toothlessly grinning at everything they saw, including us. One thing for sure, when I was growing up, the only ones who got by with going shirtless were kids like us, but only until we hit thirteen and started smelling in that new way.

And I don't mind being smiled at by strange old men. But I don't always trust it either, especially in S-Town.

Shirts and white hairy chests on reddish torsos. I saw all that, and I even waved.

I never saw whether they waved back. I should have looked, but I didn't.

§

I didn't look back because I understand how people are. I've met more friendly people in Bessemer than unkind ones. Sadly, the unkind seem to scar my memory more deeply than the friendly soothe my heart. Teenaged guys who wanted to beat the snot out of me for wearing long hair; adult family friends who said "Nigger" in front of me as often and regular as they'd say "hamburger," who expected me not to wince when they said it, and if I did, would glare as if I were about to vandalize their precious family car. I was supposed to show them respect no matter what they said, since being an adult demands an automatic deference.

Once, a family friend told me that "the Klan was right," back in the early 60's when they threatened Dr. King, and when their comrade Bull Connor unleashed the fire hoses on Black children, and then bombed and maimed little girls and old preachers. This man was an attorney. He spoke with Kennedy aides; he went to church with his family every week. He wore saddle oxfords. He spoke these words right to my face on Christmas Eve at my mother's house.

Nice manners and clothes might disguise racism and meanness for a time. But I've learned not to trust such veneers. So when we passed the porch brothers, their semi-nakedness didn't exactly worry me, though they could have been part of S-Town, the part we were looking for and afraid of finding.

The main street of West Blocton looks like that of many other old Southern towns. Except this one is really just a vestige of a time when there was a reason for the downtown. All the buildings are empty. One was an old TV repair shop, another a vacant video retailer. In fact, the only business still operating is the Cahaba Valley Lily store, which could have been a museum shop or a florist, but we didn't stop to find out. We saw a road to a school, and a strange crossroads where nothing was perpendicular or even a clear five points. Just a few roads that hardly connected, except in the way that cracked glass always has a starting point though you might not ever agree where that is.

In the "S-Town" podcast, Brian Reed talks mainly about protagonist John B. McLemore, but another figure arises as the chapters unfold. This man, Kaybram Burt, and his two sons run a lumber company in Bibb County, K3 Lumber Company. As Reed says, though there is no hard proof, the K3's could stand for the Klan, a warning or emblem to one and all. We didn't pass the lumber company, though we were on the lookout for it. We could have Googled the address, but if that thought occurred to any of us, no one chose to speak it.

We couldn't find the road to John B's house, either, because it is too obscure to be found easily, and there are many side roads like it through tall weeds that succeeded in warning us past them.

As we leave West Blocton proper, and it's almost impossible to know that you are, everything is trending away from "fine." Michael's GPS directs us toward a shorter route, and soon he yells, "Turn here," which means taking a registered, but unlined, county road. I suppose it was two-lane, but without lines, one never knows for sure. What we did know for sure is that we are soon encased by tall pines, which though beautifully lazy and even majestic, cut us off from all phone service.

--"How long will we be on this road?" Jimbo wonders.
--"It's hard to say," Michael says.
--"So, the Green Lantern scared you, but these woods are okay?"
I ask.

Michael remains quiet.

Jimbo and I begin speaking of other friends we knew, guys named Chuck, and Allen Clem, and Big Mikey. Where are they now?

This was just guy talk, masking feelings we couldn't name or admit.

We pass areas that are being clear-cut, and in one such patch of maimed woods, I see a lone deer standing, about a hundred yards away, looking right at us, as if wondering what any of us is doing here. No one but me sees the deer, and I wonder later if I really saw it, and if so, what it might have been saying to me and why it exposed itself so starkly in the cleared woods?

I suppose that K3 Lumber is responsible for defacing these woods, but before I can mention it, Jimbo says:

--"I wish we had gassed up before we started out."

We have just enough time to lose our collective breath when Jimbo starts cackling in that way he used to when he promised to buy me a Coke and returned with Dr. Pepper.

--"Not funny Jimbo," Michael says.

Since this is early August, the sun won't be setting until at least 7:30, but when you're in the woods and can't always see the sky, a different sort of darkness seeps into your brain.

--"Any service yet?" Mike asks.
--"I got a bar. It says we have maybe three or four miles to go,
and then we turn left."
--"Turn left?" Jimbo says. "Onto what?"
--"I don't know that yet. I'll keep checking."

For another five or six miles I keep assuring the car that it feels like we'll be turning soon and hitting a main road. I think about John B wanting to escape his shit town for all those years, and here I am, not making it an hour on a lonely but paved county road before beginning to worry. A Bibb County road.

I also keep thinking that if my friend Joe were with us, he'd have us back to something familiar in no time, for there's no road he's met that he hasn't called his own.

Finally, that left turn appears, and the GPS, which is back to full bars, becomes our friend again.

--"We're about thirty minutes from home," Michael says, and
just then, we enter Green Pond.
--"Should we call your folks and let them know where we are?"
--"Nah," Jimbo says. "They'll be okay."

I decide to call Joe, anyway, as much to alert someone that we aren't being held somewhere against our will as to make him understand how much I wish he had been with us.

--"Guess where we are...Green Pond!"
--"Which road?" he asks, and when I tell him I don't know but that we're passing such and such housing development, he says,

--"Oh yeah, Highway 22. I know exactly where you are."

I've heard such comforting words before, though not so many since my mother's illness and death.

After I hang up, I turn to Jimbo:

--"I'll be writing about all this one day."

He laughs, and I hear his relief.

We didn't notice any Black people in the county this day, and despite how lost we felt, no one in our car ever suggested stopping anywhere. Two gay men and two straight but half-Jewish guys—four strangers no matter how white we are--might cause some wonder, and who wants to explain what we're doing here, and why we came? I learn later that K3 Lumber is actually in Green Pond, though as we passed through that community, and I didn't see any sign. But by then, the only sign I wanted to see was for I-59 west.

§

--"No use of you running or screaming and crying
But you got a home man, long as I got mine."

It was a relief getting back on a road we vaguely knew. It isn't that I prefer interstates to back roads at all. And I've been to trailers in the woods, too, some of which might have had Confederate flags flying in front. Were these people Klansmen? Pot dealers? Crimson Tide fans?

I am not the same person as I was then, and though I still believe that I can get along with most anyone, like my mother did, I know that I can't speak for others' intentions, or from their perspectives. In situations like this riding day, my imagination wonders what would have happened if we had run out of gas or if our rented hybrid had run over a sudden log or hit one of those country pot holes and we had ended up in a ditch? Would we have been all right asking for help at one of those trailers? Would we have been treated with courtesy and respect?

And would we have deserved it, given that our journey was to find out the desperation John B felt in his shit town, the town we had not been invited to but were trespassing through anyway, seeking a thrill or a sighting of crude, desperate evil?

In the end, we didn't find anything in Bibb County except a road through some back woods that despite the clear cutting was still one of those treasures of living remotely. Even now, weeks later, I keep thinking of that deer that looked at us like we were the aliens. And we certainly were, though I like to think I was on its side. I wouldn't eradicate its habitat, nor would I hunt it down. That isn't how I was raised, and I'm not judging here. Just stating the way it is and always was.

About hunting, the woods, and the people there.

About what I know and believe.

Last week, I told my therapist, about that deer, and he read to me from *Animals Speak*:

"The deer...reminds us to establish a strong healthy connection with the child before we expose it to many people and other strange energies. It is a reminder that there is a tradition that is natural and suitable for family units and for the health of the young. It is for the child's best interest...it is all the rule of the mother...if the deer has shown up in your life...you have gotten too far away from the role that would be most beneficial for you at this time...Anyone who has a deer as a totem will find increasing ability to detect subtle movements and appearances. They will begin to hear what may not be said directly. When deer show up in your life it is time to be gentle with yourself and others. A new innocence and freshness is about to be awakened or born. There is going to be a gentle, enticing lure of new adventures....an opportunity to express gentle love that will open new doors to adventure for you" (263-4).

Though I heard these words now, in that driving moment, all I saw was a lone creature, and I feared for its safety, which, given our vulnerability, might have been a projection.

And speaking of vulnerability, I also realize that on her trips measuring trailers and cabins and sub-developed homes, my mother relied on the verbal directions given her—you know, things like, "When you get to the sign that says New Bethel Baptist, turn right and go for a good ways, and then you'll see the fence to our property." Surely she had a county map to help, but maps can't keep up with someone's rutting a new road out of Alabama red clay. Way out in this country, there are few clearly marked addresses, yet she always found her destination.

Mom didn't have a phone either; no one did back then. Sometimes her colleague, Ollie, rode with her, but most of the time she went alone, trusting that both her drive and the results would stand her in good stead, give her a needed commission, or at least a story to tell over supper.

She took these chances for my brother and me. In fact, she gave up her dream of owning an antique shop and accepted a retail job--which she hated and which, because of the heavy sample cases she had to load and unload, permanently displaced a disc in her back--because a sales job would earn her more income to help put my brother and me through college. Whether she wanted us to escape this land or not, she hoped we'd make more of ourselves than she ever could. One of the last things she told me was,

--"My only hope and wish for you and Mike was that you'd get an education and make something of your life. And you did."

Maybe, given the potholes, the narrow winding roads, and the lack of barriers on unlit turns for miles and miles, there's a reason for all those car graveyards in "S-Town." Maybe I should think harder about places we travel through on whims and larks. Maybe I should be grateful that my mother, my friends, and I understand to the extent we do the pains and joys of life up in this county, this USA. There is a joy in feeling assured that the road you're on, as lost as you might believe you are, will lead to a place you know and understand.

As we crisscrossed through rough and unfamiliar land, I kept seeing my past self and those who shaped me—particularly my parents—navigating our lives, doing what we loved and what we had to do to go on living well and meaningfully, for ourselves and for each other.

Feeling so unsettled before our journey that day, so adrift in grief, so unmoored from my center, by the journey's end, I realized that this afternoon, especially with my best friend, was a way of finding home in a place that I'd known about but never experienced before. For it's the experiences we share, layering the new ones on top of a lifetime of others, which renew our bonds and keep us living through our loss.

It's been two months since my mother passed, and my trips back to Bessemer are numbered. Going back to settle her home, I can't help following her steps:

--"There's Durwood's house,"

I say even when I'm alone and even though someone else likely lives there now since Durwood passed last fall.

--"And there's the man with those little horses."

Is OCD passed through our genes? Can we breathe it in and get addicted like the lingering of secondhand smoke? A lifelong smoker, my mother quit after they found a spot of cancer in her lung five years ago. It wasn't the lung that got her, though, but her liver. From diagnosis to death in under two weeks.

Summer is fading, and college football's season is five weeks old. I still have a package of summer peas in the freezer, which one day this fall, I'll thaw and cook for my wife and me, and then I'll tell her this story, about what I saw on our road trip. And what I'll never see again.

A deer alone in the clear-cut woods, looking at me, and calling my name.

# Darkened Churches

David Joy writes realistically violent novels, mainly set in the Appalachian region of western North Carolina. One of the bloodier moments in his second novel, *The Weight of This World*, concerns a returned Afghani War vet who exacts revenge on a man who has skewered the vet's dog. The vet forces this killer on an extended last trek through the mountains.

And on that death march, the vet uses a tactic he learned from his wartime enemy: before the march begins, he takes a sharp knife and carves off the soles of the killer's feet. It makes the walking excruciating, but still possible.

A character who enacts this sort of violent revenge has to be single-minded and obsessed by red-hot passion, right? We can't like him or appreciate the rest of him, can we? Well, not exactly true. We have to take him as wholly as we can; we have to be willing to see what he sees and consider the meanings of his past, triggered by his observations.

For instance, just before this character makes another irrevocable decision, he arrives at a scene he's contemplated before, but never this deeply or from this particular vantage:

He studied the church, just a plain white clapboard building with brick steps leading to the door, no front windows, a steeple holding its cross into the sky. From the outside it was like most churches in Jackson County, the only difference being that this was where he'd been baptized, once shortly after he was born and once years later...Soon after the church bells rang, the church deacon, Samuel Mathis, opened the front door and the congregation filed out. Children were the first down the steps. Little girls in cotton dresses and patent-leather shoes strung daisy chains in the grass, while boys yanked their shirttails loose and chased one another around the building. The older kids huddled into circles. Teenage girls pulled out their cell phones to text one another. They snickered as they glanced back at boys the same age who kicked the dirt with the toes of their shoes and told lies that Thad could read in their gestures. Middle-aged men helped widows down the stairs while the men's wives desperately tried to round up their kids and corral them into the cars. The older couples were always the last to leave. They stood hunched over and slowly grazed their way around the gravel on canes until all their good-byes had been said. Only then did they drive away to lonely farms that no longer had crops to grow. They'd eat their Sunday suppers and wait for Wednesday service, and when the day came that they were widowed, they'd take their meals alone" (219-20).

It's not just that this is a sad, melancholy passage, though God knows, it is. It's that these images are so carefully rendered that if the author himself has never noticed such scenes, I'll be damned.

The peace that passeth all understanding makes me shiver as I think of all that this scene suggests. The kids, sure, and the middle-aged parents—they're painted clearly and with truth.

But the elderly couples, the ones who keep coming every week, twice a week, reinforcing, or is it still seeking, their saving grace, their redemption? Do they know what has been happening in their midst: the drugs, the abuse, the torture, and waste? Are they oblivious to these realities? We don't know because Joy is being suggestive here; we can peer closer at this sketch if we want, but he won't fill in any more ground.

Still, we consider these couples' end—our own end; they wither on their vine and die one by one. If they have consolation, we don't see it, for as much as they are a part of their community and this church, their death will be alone, if not lonely, and unadorned. When they die, the church will surely embrace them again, and that is a comfort to some.

I keep seeing them: the last to leave as they "graze" through the "gravel parking lot," and "tak[e] their meals alone." I wonder who has cooked, what they'll eat, and who'll clean up? There are sadder things than an elderly person eating alone, but right now, I don't want to know what they are.

§

My father passed in December 2000. My mother lived until she was eighty-five, so for the last eighteen years, she took her meals mainly alone. Sometimes she'd have a friend over for supper; sometimes she'd go out to a local restaurant with a group, and at other times, she'd go to her church's monthly Family Night supper. I figure that she ate 6500+ suppers in that time since my father died. In 2003, when she began keeping company with another good man by the name of Vines, she probably cooked for him once or twice a week (roast beef and summer vegetables; winter stews and vegetable soup and cornbread). He certainly escorted her out to eat regularly, be it Ruby Tuesday, Cracker Barrel, or her favorite, Bessemer's Bright Star, where the fresh red snapper from the Gulf of Mexico reigns supreme. Mr. Vines passed away in the summer of 2016, so estimating her suppers alone gets trickier. Counting those occasions plus times my family and my brother visited her, I figure that she took close to 5500 nightly meals alone, either at the table or, increasingly, in her recliner in front of MSNBC or the HG Network.

Sometimes when my wife travels with friends, I spend three or four night at home on my own. The first night might be a taste of freedom: I can eat a frozen pizza; I can binge on a violent Netflix series like "Ozark;" I can leave the dishes till morning. By the second night, I'm bored, and on the third, quite lonely, though my dog Max sleeps by my side. In these alone times, I hope, selfishly, that I'll die first, many years from now.

In the months before my mother's death, her church friends kept special watch over her. They called frequently, rescued her when her heart went racing, when she contracted pneumonia, and when, at the end, she couldn't understand why she had no appetite and felt so weak. Her family was with her at the end, and we saw how her church supported her and us. Embraced us, even though neither my wife, nor my daughters and I qualify as "believers" any longer.

My mother's church saw to it that we had a meal before the funeral, and after. Friends kept taking us out to eat or bringing food as we began the process of clearing her house for sale. I kept her TV and recliner till the end, and her supper table. My wife and I gave my parents that kitchen table almost thirty years ago, an unfinished piece of pine wood that we had clear-stained.

While it was difficult to let these things go, it was also comforting to keep what her church meant to her and to us.

I let the church have her table and chairs, her recliner and sofa, the TV. Someone who needs them will enjoy these last things, and my mother would have wanted it this way. I like to think it's a young family that will gather round her table for fried chicken or roast beef suppers; a middle-aged couple that will share that sofa, reading together on rainy nights; and perhaps another widow or widower who will relax in her chair in front of Mom's TV, listening to voices of comedy or home improvement.

This is what happens with what we have at the end; it disperses, the original owner forgotten, if ever known.

Yet, as natural as this process is, how do I let go of what I gave freely? How do I close out a house, and say goodbye, especially when I keep this image?

Each night from my home two states away, I saw my mother eating her soup and crackers, or simply scooping Palmetto Cheese up with Town House crackers—one of her favorite meals--later finishing with a container of Haagen-Dazs Coffee ice cream.

All alone.

§

Not long ago as my wife, my brother-in-law, and I were returning from a Jim Lauderdale concert at The Spinning Jenny in Greer, SC, we passed a beautiful old church on the main thoroughfare into town. This was a Saturday night, about 11:15. The church exterior was well lit, but I could see that inside, not unexpectedly, everything was dark, awaiting the next morning when the doors would let in scores of families for morning worship.

"Seeing a dark church late at night has always creeped me out," I said.

When I was a kid, what I would have meant by "creeped out" was that I feared being locked alone in a church late at night. The darkened Sunday School rooms throughout a four-story structure including the basement. All those hallways with their shiny linoleum floors. What if, all alone, I heard footsteps? Worse, what if I made my way to the sanctuary and instead of a large cross hanging over the pulpit, I saw something else, shadowy and moving?

Once, our youth group held a lock-in, where we were supposed to spend an entire Friday night in the church till morning, some adult nearby just in case. I grew up in this church; it seems we always had some business there, and and my grandmother used to cook in the basement kitchen for church meetings. Yet something happened to me this night. Some thought I had a stomach virus; others contended it was the fish sticks we cooked in the church's gas oven. Maybe they weren't fully heated. In any case, I had to be driven home and missed whatever fun or adventures or moving specters were to come. I ran a fever the next day and had to cancel my first-ever date, but as I considered the cause of my illness, I wondered whether my illness wasn't all fear-based, a dark closeness to some other end?

On the night we drove home from the music, though, my feelings weren't conditioned by a young boy's supernatural visions. I felt sad, alone. True, it had been only two months since my mother passed.

"What do you mean?" my wife asked. "Creeped out how?"

"Like there should always be someone there, someone living there. Empty churches at night make me want to cry."

I didn't know how to explain this to my wife. I don't even know how to explain it to myself. I'm not dying to attend church even though my mother's church filled a hole in me and not just on the day of her funeral.

There were two or three Fourth of July nights when the church held its Independence Day hamburger/hot dog suppers. I accompanied my mother to these banquet-room galas where we'd eat too many grilled sandwiches, revel in the homemade ice cream, watch the children's parade, and then head out to the parking lot for the fireworks display, my mother wanting us to sit as close under the sky explosions as we could.

My mother joined this church, Pleasant Hill United Methodist on the outskirts of Bessemer, in 2010, after First Methodist, the church of both our youths, closed its doors once its congregants dwindled to single digits. The building was badly in need of repair, too, and no one could afford to renovate it.

I quit believing long ago, but twice since she joined Pleasant Hill, I joined her for Sunday services. The first was an Easter service, and I accompanied Mom more to soothe her soul than to save mine. It didn't hurt me to listen to the message of resurrection. More than anything, as the children sang, and the other congregants welcomed me, I felt calm, peaceful.

The other time was for the Christmas service year before last, an all-musical affair. How long had it been since I sang en masse "God Rest Ye Merry Gentlemen," "It Came Upon a Midnight Clear," or my favorite, "Good King Wenceslas?"

Attending didn't change my outlook, my disbelief, my way of looking at religion. I even thought that if I didn't have to accept Jesus as Savior, I could go more often. But I'm no hypocrite, and I know that I don't have the feeling inside me. So how do I understand my sadness at seeing any church alone, empty inside?

Last night I read an essay in *The Oxford American* about the author's exploration of Eastern Orthodox Christianity:

> "...as I've moved around the country for my career, the Orthodox faith has remained at the center of my life...I now belong to the OCA cathedral in Manhattan's East Village, a place with an illustrious century-plus history and the most diverse Orthodox congregation I've ever found. It's more a home to me than my own apartment is; the community there is my surrogate family"

(Nick Tabor, "The Light of Salvation," *The Oxford American,* Fall 2018, 88).

I could say the same about many in my mother's church, not only because they are longtime family friends, but just as plainly because they gave me that safe feeling of acceptance and love, by continuing to embrace my mother, by making those lonely nights seem less so, for her and for me. They know my name, of course, what I do, and what I don't believe. And in their knowing, they never once tried to convince me of anything except how much they love us.

My mother's church shows such love in other ways, too. The preacher himself has taken in several homeless children, adopted them as his own, despite their ongoing problems. His house is bursting, or so I hear.

This makes me wonder: why can't homeless families live in the church, supervised by rotating church officials? Why can't the kitchens operate for all meals, and beyond the homeless, why can't any widow take her meals there whenever she wants? Why can't the lonely couples go on other nights besides Sundays and Wednesdays? Why is Family Night only once a month?

As a kid, I wondered why the preacher didn't live at the church instead of the parsonage next door? Couldn't this man of God keep the flames inside the church alive by being there all the time?

I still wonder this now.

I know, if I hate seeing abandoned people and lonely places, why don't I donate my own funds to aid this cause? I'm still working on my own answers. Thinking about my own contemplative scenes.

§

When I was a child, I had to be forced to go church, and no Sunday service ever gave me peace. I left the church of my youth when I moved away to college. I never really missed it, either.

Except.

When I think back on how my church affected me, even though I can't accept Jesus as Savior or deal with his torturous execution, I realize that it taught me the desire to do good works, and to seek peace. I don't remember all the lessons thrust at me, and many of the ones I do are blood-drenched epochs of annihilation and transformation. Still, there's "The Good Samaritan," and my favorite, the fish and the loaves of bread.

Jesus feeding multitudes, who all ate together, who all had enough to share with each other, who all were taught how to give what they have to ensure that no one goes hungry, is cast off, or left abandoned and alone.

And I remember the only other part of church I loved, the hymns. I sang in the choir at night and on some mornings. Even sitting in the congregation otherwise bored, I joined in every song.

I thought of those times last night when my wife and I were watching "The Andy Griffith Show." It was the episode where an impatient travelling businessman gets stranded in Mayberry on a Sunday. No one can pacify the man who can't see the value, but only the quirks, of this pastoral place. As day moves to evening and he awaits the Pyle brothers to fix his finely-tuned car, the man sits on the Taylor porch, rocking, and listening to Andy and Barney sing an old song.

"The Church in the Wildwood."

"Oh come come come come. Come to the Church in the Wildwood. Come to the Church in the vale. No place is as dear to my childhood, as the little brown church in the vale."

Maybe it's only nostalgia. Even when you don't believe like everyone else in the congregation, home is home, this place of your childhood, this church of your youth, your middle years or your old age.

As I now re-read David Joy's passage, I see myself in those who congregate outside the church after service: the little boys "yanking loose their shirttails;" the older kids "huddled together;" the middle-aged men and women helping others and their own; and especially the last couple who leaves, whom everyone believes is happy and comfortable; whom no one worries about.

This passage is not a lamentation or even a wakeup call. It's just an observable moment taken from a character who has never known peace.

I think my mother should have the last word. Whenever she felt sorry for someone, or considered afflictions of body, mind, or material travail, or when she just got exasperated with the ravings of our current president, she'd let out a sighing but sometimes caustic, "Lord Have Mercy." This phrase, I learned, is something the congregants say after almost every sentence that an Eastern Orthodox priest speaks [Tabor 86].

It's something I believe David Joy would say in benediction for all the wayward, lonely, and forgotten souls in his particular Babylon.

True and soothing words of grace.

# Secrets I'm Dying to Tell You

When I published my second book of essays, my mother commented that I had "told all her secrets now." But that wasn't true; neither she nor I had revealed them all yet.

I write this in the aftermath of the Brett Kavanaugh/Christine Blasey Ford trauma. We know whose story the majority of the Senate Judiciary Committee believes, and many of us are not surprised. But do we know how Kavanaugh explained his actions to his daughter? Has he told her what sexual assault means?

I am deeply troubled by so many aspects of this story including, and maybe most of all, what this little girl will now live through and with. Her father and his story.

One question people are asking is why Dr. Blasey Ford waited thirty-six years to tell her story. People who ask such questions might never have been victims themselves, but I can't claim to know what motivates their wondering. I've never told how I was a victim of a would-be sexual

predator either, and I'm a sixty-something-year-old white man. I have my reasons, so I imagine Dr. Blasey Ford has hers, many of which we're seeing hypothesized in print these days.

But back to my mother and the printing of her secrets and dying days.

§

Exactly a week before she died, my mother sat in her hospital bed entertaining her troops—her legion of family and friends who seemingly couldn't get enough of her stories; her prescriptions on life and how to live it; her pronouncements as to who and what were "just plain stupid."

We—my wife, two daughters, and brother—had again fallen victim to her "stupid" indictment. Mom had liver cancer, and though she knew she was terminal, she didn't know how long she had left. Nor did she know that her oncologist had told us that Mom would likely die this very Saturday, not knowing, of course, that it is in my mother's nature—and perhaps in that of every Southern woman of her generation—not to heed any doctor's warning or label and, in fact, to spite whatever pronouncement they might make.

"I just hate doctors," she told everyone after she had undergone a lung biopsy earlier that year that came back negative. "They just put you through hell!"

So spite can prolong life for an indeterminate time.

We who still treat doctors as gods knew that her time was limited, though. When we'd return to her house at night for whatever hours' sleep we could grab, none of us had the heart to sleep in Mom's bed. Of course, each morning when we'd return to the hospital, she'd ask us two series of questions:

"What did y'all have her breakfast? Did you find the sweet potato bread I had frozen, or the sausages and bacon?"

"Yes ma'am, we did," and though my wife had actually eaten her standard fruit and yogurt, enough of us had enjoyed the food Mom left that we felt our answer to be truthful and satisfying.

It was our answer to her second question that incurred her wrath:

"Now, where did y'all sleep last night? I hope someone slept in my bed!"

Our sheepish smiles told her everything.

"Well, Mike [my brother] slept in the back bedroom, Pari and Layla [our daughters] on the fold-out couch, and Nilly [my wife] and I slept on the air mattress," I confessed.

Mom looked at us just like we had decided to touch an electrified fence.

"Well, that's just stupid. You have that big comfortable bed with the Pillowtop mattress, and no one slept in it? And instead the two of you slept on an air mattress? Why, that's the stupidest thing I ever heard!"

She was as mad and exasperated with us as I've ever seen her.

I wonder now: on this day when she was "supposed" to die, did our foolishness keep her going? It must have, as she proceeded to castigate us to all the friends who began dropping by her room at 10 that morning and kept dropping by until 8 that evening. One of her friends told us that Mom's minister Alan Head, who came by that afternoon, reported the next morning from his pulpit that Mom's room was one big party:

"From the minute you get off the elevator, you see a line stretching all the way down the hall from her room. I believe I even saw the Chippendale dancers waiting to get in!" he joked.

My mother loved Rev. Head, and allowed him to pray for her that Saturday.

"Just don't go on like that chaplain who came in here yesterday did," she told him. "I thought that man was never going to leave! I'm sure he was a Baptist."

"Don't worry," Rev. Head said. "I'm going to give you a good old Methodist prayer, about ten seconds' worth."

That he might have pushed his blessing to fifteen seconds caused none of us, even the non-believers, any concern.

What I'm saying is that despite what we knew, despite how full of sorrow we were, and despite the reality facing us if not this day, then one day soon, we were thankful, and, yes, blessed to have this time with my mother. I remember saying to everyone who asked about Mom's prognosis:

"We really don't know how long we have, so I am just enjoying this moment, and the ones to come. If I've learned anything about this process, it's that none of us knows anything about it."

I knew my mother was not going to beat this disease. She was eighty-five and even if it would have helped, she had refused chemotherapy. Still, when I looked over all the people who loved her, I felt as though these moments of peace, of bliss, might last forever.

The night before, our first hospice nurse had visited. Ron was a kind man, and he took my brother and me to another room where we could fill out the paperwork and talk quietly. He offered us information about hospice services and promised to make this part of life as painless, as kind, and as loving as possible. His wife, Kim—also a hospice nurse—came the next morning to examine Mom, and she told me afterward that she didn't think Mom was "imminent."

"She looks good, actually," Kim said.

Again, this was Saturday, the day her oncologist had predicted Mom would pass. So after Kim's examination, I had every reason to think that we had many good days left, perhaps even weeks. Understandably, I felt better than I had since Mom's diagnosis four days earlier. I felt something like joy.

And then Hell, otherwise known as a new hospice nurse, ascended.

Because I am a polite Southern man, I won't name this woman. What I can say is that while I was standing in the hallway waiting on a nurse's aide to finish giving my mother a sponge bath, this new hospice nurse appeared out of nowhere, walked over to me, and after briefly introducing herself, launched into the reason for her visit.

"Your mother is now in respite care, which means that you have five days to decide what to do with her. She has to leave the hospital after that time and either go home or go into another facility. That's the government talking, not me."

She might have reiterated this message two or three times, as if I were dumb. As if, somehow, I wasn't grieving and in a semi-state of shock.

"You're going to have to decide and come up with a plan by Monday."

So much for the peace that passes all understanding.

Her work wasn't done, however.

"Now I'm going in to see your mother and do my voodoo on her."

At that point she was joined by the hospice case manager and by the hospital's social worker; each spoke much more graciously and compassionately to us. Yet when they finally had all left us, I felt complete despair.

It was only after she left that my mother reported one other chapter of this voodoo woman's hellish mouth:

"She asked me what religious denomination I belonged to, and when I told her I was a Methodist, she said, 'Well I'm a Baptist. Don't you know that Baptists are the best?'"

Maybe there is room for levity when a woman lies dying. But not from a stranger, and definitely not from someone whose main calling is to convey compassion and care.

"Oh Mom, I'm so sorry." And then I added my own lightness, for I have that right, "If only you had a copy of my book with you!"

"Yeah, that would have shown her!"

My mother had inspired the title of my first essay collection: "*Don't Date Baptists and Other Warnings From My Alabama Mother*," the advisory being something she had told me when I was fourteen and considering the world of girls. I did date some Baptists, though, and if she minded, she never directly said.

On the next day I called the hospice office and formally complained about this worker and her manner—her way of making us feel threatened, harassed, like we were being evicted alone and helpless into some netherworld.

"If she ever returns," I said, "I will personally bar her from getting close to my mother."

The manager assured me that we'd never see this woman again, that she had "too much on her plate" that day and shouldn't have been sent out in the first place. She was "old school and spoke her mind." Later, another hospice nurse told me that this old school voodoo nurse's mouth had gotten her into trouble before, yet not enough trouble to keep her from being foisted upon us.

We never saw that worker again, and everyone else who came from that agency, especially Jennifer and Holly, provided just what we needed: comfort and care, honesty and compassion. I wish, though, that all their care could have undone those few moments of terror on the Saturday my mother was supposed to die.

However, terror finds its way to us at any time, regardless of our emotional state, regardless of proper decorum or etiquette.

And especially regardless of whether we believe we are living in a place of refinement, proper manners, and the best breeding. Old southern charm and "our way of life down here," are only words on a page, after all.

§

"Grandma, tell us about the strangest thing that ever happened to you!"

On this supposedly fated Saturday night, I started to say to my daughters, "Be careful what you ask for," especially if the person you're asking is your grandmother who loves to tell stories and who, in her dying days, might be especially uncensored.

"The strangest thing that ever happened to me? Hmm. Well, I guess it was when I was at Ramsay High School and was walking home one day. I was walking down Highland Avenue and this boy I knew, though I didn't know him well, pulled alongside me and offered me a ride. I shouldn't have gone, but I did. He was one of those blacks...."

At this point I couldn't think straight. First, for the last thirty years or so, Mom has referred to African-American people as "blacks," a term she might have found inoffensive, but which always made me wince. The only other group she lumped into one category no matter the individual was the

Baptists. Understand: I am not apologizing for her; these were her views, her life.

Though my mind reeled with this decades-old insult, I still couldn't process my mother getting in the car with a Black man, circa 1948/49.

"Well, we rode for a ways, past the turn to my house. 'Where are we going?' I asked, but he wouldn't say anything. And then he suddenly pulled over off the side of the road. Before I knew it, he was on me. He was one of the *Blach's*."

And then it hit me.

"Do you mean 'one of the Blach's' like the department store Blach's?"

"Yes, like I said, one of the Blach's."

Blach's was one of Birmingham's oldest and most prestigious businesses. Its store trademark logo, which the family registered, was "Fair and Square." About the emblem accompanying this logo:

> 'First you see the circle, indicative of [the] endless power of good within. Second, you see the lily, indicative of purity. Third, you see the green leaf, indicative of everlasting life. Fourth, you see the square, indicative of true dealing. Then taking the lily in its fair whiteness and combining it with the square, you produce the well-known motto of this firm—Fair and Square—which has not a blot of unjust dealing against it' (Hollis, *Memories of Downtown Birmingham*, 19-20).

Of course, for decades and into the 1960's, Blach's engaged in complete racial segregation, as did all of downtown Birmingham's retail stores, so "unjust" is entirely relative and subjective. Considering the earnestness of the emblem and its description, however, what my mother said next is particularly disturbing:

"Before I knew it, he came at me, and he had a pair of those dental braces dentists use to pry your mouth open while they do a filling. He stuck that brace in my mouth!"

"What did you do, Grandma?"

"I fought him off. Finally, I was able to get out of that car before he did anything else. I tell you, he was some kind of sadist."

"Did you ever tell anyone about what happened, Grandma?"

"No, I never did. Oh, maybe I told one of my friends back then, but no one else. Not until now."

Using the Google search engine, my daughter Layla tried looking up the name of this Blach boy, but she had no luck. Besides, time was running out on this night, and we all wanted to talk more. The stories turned lighter, and my daughters recorded everything Mom said on their iPhones. They had her say all her "southernisms"—"Bless your heart," "Lord have Mercy"—and they even had her shout a big "Roll Tide."

It's hard to forget trauma, though, even and perhaps especially seventy-year old trauma.

As I lay in the hospital cot next to Mom that night, and lying next to me, Layla, who didn't want me to watch alone, I kept thinking of my mother as a naïve young girl, too trusting for her own good. It's strange, indeed, what happened to her. I wouldn't allow my mind then to contemplate just what this boy planned to do once he had my mother's mouth pried open. Now, I can't make my imagination stop.

Once when I was a boy, I overheard my grandmother telling one of her friends that my Mom "just isn't kissable." I must have been nine or ten, and I wondered what that meant, how my grandmother would know. Now, maybe I understand.

Less than three years after this assault, however, my mother met and fell in love with my father. She was eighteen, and he, twenty-five. They were married forty-eight years.

I coupled this scene of my mother's near rape with another incident she had told me about: a boy she was on a date with also tried to rape her in a remote Birmingham setting. She escaped and had to walk alone through downtown Birmingham late at night before she found a cab. According to her, she managed to get away before the very worst happened. That the worst could have happened; that I might not know everything about these incidents; that there might be other incidents keeps me from sleeping well.

I think one of the worst things I can imagine and envision is my mother, a girl alone, vulnerable and innocent, being treated in the worst possible way. She did her best to protect me, but who protected her?

In one of our last conversations alone, I was telling my mother how I never wanted to be parted from her, how when I was a boy, my bouts of homesickness when I spent the night with friends were due to missing her.

"I was the same way when I was a little girl," she told me. "Once, I was spending the night across the street with Emily Staub, and I got to missing my mother so badly that I just got up and ran across the street home. I was just a little girl."

As a boy in kindergarten, I had to recite with my class every morning the 23rd Psalm. When we got to the part about "walking through the valley of the shadow of death," I'd start crying, every day. No teacher could ever extract from me why I cried. No one made the connection between verse and my tears at all, and I couldn't tell them what I saw when I heard those words.

Until kindergarten, I was with my mother every day, and on many of these days, we'd walk down the sidewalk in our neighborhood, our shadows looming in front or behind, as the sun goes. Sometimes, Mom would pick up a rock or a stick to ward off unfriendly dogs, holding my hand all the while. I always feared the one place at the end of the block: a vacant lot bordered by high, untended shrubs, which anyone could have been lurking behind. I imagined that after I went to kindergarten, she'd walk down the street alone, without me, and whatever comfort or protection I could provide.

That was when I'd cry, when I saw her all alone.

Two days after the deadline hospice had issued for leaving the hospital, from some quarter of my brain, I saw my sidewalk path clearly.

My mother still looked good, and if we had to go somewhere, it would be to her home. Though I had to get a hospital bed, I could put her sheets and pillows on it. There is a comfort in home even when it's bound to be your dying place. Leaving the hospital that late morning, Mom dressed up again, complete with makeup and lipstick. She would never go anywhere looking like she had just gotten out of bed, like she was sick or alone, vulnerable or dying.

She lived another four days, spending most of that time in bed or in her recliner. She took to that chair, her favorite in the house, where she watched her "programs" like "Chicago Fire," "Law and Order: SVU," and MSNBC's lineup of progressive news. She particularly loved Chris Hayes' "Thing 1 and Thing 2," and of course, Rachel Maddow. The darkness of the Trump era revved Mom up, and her dearest hope was to live to see "that stupid fool" impeached or otherwise gotten rid of.

I know what she would have thought of the Kavanaugh affair. I can hear her now saying, "Such a disgrace."

And I'd understand that for her, this wasn't just politics. Like many other women I know, this assault was her awful reality.

My wife, my brother, our good friend Sallie, and I were with her until the end—comforting her, helping her walk into that valley, as she departed us.

I thought about trying to find the man who hurt her, the one who forced a dentist's vise on her. He'd be in his late 80's now, if he's still alive. I thought about doing more research into his family, even contacting them. But what would be the point? I couldn't prove anything, and the victim herself can't tell her story. I am even taking a risk by naming the predator as far as I have.

A man named Blach, from a once-prominent Birmingham family.

That's all I know, and it will never be enough. But I believe it happened. I believe my mother. Like in the other #MeToo cases I've heard, I know that there is nothing to be gained from her making this story up. I know that in this memory, my mother was definitely not "mixed-up."

A couple of weeks after the Kavanaugh confirmation, I was discussing with my Intro to Literature students an act of violence against a woman in Chris Offut's novel, *Country Dark*. One of my male students asked if I thought things were turning around now, meaning that women were now gaining the upper hand by falsely accusing men of rape and other acts of violence or by waiting so long to accuse these men that no one can prove whether the act actually occurred or not.

"No," I said. "I don't believe things are 'turning around.' Kavanaugh is now a justice, and Dr. Ford has been ridiculed by many, including the President."

I didn't stop there, however; I decided to tell my mother's story. Maybe she wouldn't have wanted me to. But given the stunned silence that followed this telling, I think I did the right thing.

"That's nearly seventy years she waited before telling this story," I said. "She figured no one would believe her, or that telling would cause trouble for her family given that his was so socially prominent."

As I continue to tell her strange secret, I don't feel so alone now. But I do feel the sorrow, the emptiness, and need to make sense of all that happened to her. To us. To rely on the goodness and mercy that she gave me and that I hope I returned to her, every day of her life, and especially when she felt as alone as I once did.

# Basement Confidential

What is the strangest room in your house?

When we first moved into our current house, I might have said my daughters' bedroom, which had a false door from a previously conceived layout, and a secret cabinet in the closet, where someone in later years stashed her "weed." That room is now our master suite, no strange or identifying markers left. Only memories.

Then there's the house of my youth: a simple structure built in the 1920's, one story, with a basement that has a door and a finished room under the stairs, existing for an unknowable reason, floating next to the unfinished majority basement space that contained sewage and other pipes leading to the front of the house where darkened corners held traps of poisoned peanut butter sandwiches for the rats that most old houses "house."

When my parents sold that house in 1996, the finished basement room held Dad's three lawn mowers—two power, and one old-fashioned hand-pushed—his rakes, shovels, edgers, leaf blower, wheelbarrow, various old buckets, and several pairs of lawn/hedge clippers. Our front lawn was split into four quadrants, together comprising an area of perhaps a single tennis court including alleys. Dad saw the yard as the natural gateway to his castle. He moved in when he married my mother in 1952 and inherited a black tool chest from Mom's father, and the hammers, screwdrivers, braces and bits that went with it. Though that chest rested in our bathroom hall closet for most of its life, it eventually found its way to that basement room.

In those latter years before my parents moved, our basement room also contained Dad's cardio-vascular exercise equipment, or rather, his archaic stationary bike, which had no computer, only a speedometer and mileage gauge. Though you could adjust the seat level, nothing you could do would cushion the firmness of that seat. Riding that bike was never pleasant since maybe fifteen minutes into the exercise, at least one half of my butt would fall asleep. Dad claimed that this never happened to him, but

I also noticed on those occasions when I came for visits, that the mileage gauge hadn't moved all that much since my last ride. I could go almost four miles in an hour, and the last I saw of the bike, it had maybe fifty miles on it. Dad said he preferred walking in the fresh air, and I couldn't blame him, given that to ride in our basement room also meant breathing in its stale, musty air.

Our basement room had one window looking out onto the side of the house where my parents kept a series of barbeque grills sitting on concrete-tiled stones. So while the window afforded some view, it also afforded anyone on the outside an equal view right into our finished basement room—not a problem unless you wanted to hide Christmas bicycles from your children, thinking they wouldn't be snooping around. Thinking two boys ages six and ten had anything like self-control or awareness about them.

Three different doors offered access to that basement room. The door most often used was the one leading from the basement stairs, a staircase accessed upstairs from our breakfast room. Those stairs were original to the house--wooden with faded green paint. I hated using them because there was no railing on one side. My childhood cat, Tom, used to sit on the pipe to the immediate left of the upper step, a place accessed from gaps in the exterior structure of the house, climbing, as the rats did, to the upper level. I don't remember why, but that staircase door to the finished basement room was always kept shut, as if someone needed to be kept out, as if someone might need privacy.

The room extended about twenty feet. At its entrance, you'd notice the second door, which was the original exterior door to this room, leading out and down two steps to the original back yard. It was two doors, actually: the wooden main door, and a screen door attached. When I was four years old, the left side of our house—the opposite side of this basement room— caught on fire. We lived at the Holiday Inn for the next month, while not only the burned part of our house was restored, but a new edition added: a new bedroom and bathroom for my parents, and a den. To add these three rooms, part of the original back yard had to be enclosed; thus, we had a door from our basement room that led pretty much nowhere except to another dirt basement floor. I don't remember the door before the fire; after, though, I wanted to use it as often as I could.

What is it about doors leading to nowhere?

My parents never removed either the wooden or the screen door for as long as they lived in that house, but after 1968 or so, those two doors were never opened again.

The third door to our finished basement room was an addition cut out in the mid 1970's when my mother decided to open her own antique shop, Jo's Antiques. She was carrying on a tradition started by her mother who owned antique shops in various locations across Bessemer for years.

Jo's Antiques was my mother's attempt to help pay for my brother's and my college tuition. It lasted only a year, though, and then Mom took a job selling carpet, retail. But while it lasted, Jo's Antiques had a sign plaqued onto its top archway. After it closed, Dad had a concrete ramp installed and then moved his lawn equipment from the dirty part of the basement to that finished room.

My brother reminded me recently that it was he and our neighbor, Frank Manzella, who cut out the third door and laid the new flooring in that basement room for Jo's Antiques. A few years earlier, the old wooden floor had completely rotted out, a fact we discovered one afternoon while playing down there as teenagers when after one heavy step, my foot went entirely through the floorboards.

Before my foot discovered the rotted flooring, I had been hoping that this room would become my teenage refuge—a place not only to escape my parents' eyes and ears so that I could talk freely on the phone and listen to "my music," but also one I might decorate in mod styles and use as my bedroom.

My refuge would have been perfect because in the back part of the room there was a private bathroom—just a toilet and a sink—but they worked fine. We know they worked fine because there were two reasons why the wooden floor rotted. The first reason was termites, which certainly did their damage. They were complemented, however, on a winter's day in 1966, by either a sewer pipe above bursting, or the toilet itself overflowing. My mother actually used both descriptions. I have never known exactly what happened, why or how it happened. What I do know is that prior to this calamity, my mother insisted that my brother and I store our comic book and baseball card collection down there.

In cardboard boxes.

I keep thinking about this time in all its complicated avenues. We had two functioning bathrooms upstairs, so why would anyone go downstairs to use that basement toilet? With my brother and me at school, that left only my mother, my grandmother, and our maid Dissie at home. Could all three have needed to use the bathroom at the same time? And given the dust, the rats, the normal load of spiders and roaches, why would anyone willingly traverse those steps in any non-emergency bathroom need?

But I wonder: my comics and cards were stacked at least three feet high in their boxes. Could the sewage really have risen that high? Couldn't any of them have been rescued? Couldn't someone have stuck a hand into a pile of comics and grabbed the top ones—the ones unlikely to have been damaged, giving me something to cherish? Who hauled it all away, and how did they accomplish all of this before I got home from school?

And why was I not allowed to go down there and look? Did we understand the nature of biohazards back in 1966?

Was my mother telling me the truth back then about that toilet, or did she simply want to free up space in that room for something else? Maybe she was tired of all the "junk" that was accumulating. Or maybe the pipe did burst.

My mother passed last summer, so I'm reluctant to cast such aspersions. Yet, she hated clutter, and she did throw away old games, toys, and anything else that seemed in the way—after first consigning them to open bins in the unfinished, dirt part of the basement.

§

My earliest memory of our finished basement room was my mother's art studio. Every Saturday morning she faithfully watched Jon Gnagy's "Learn to Draw" NBC TV show, and soon bought one of his beginner's kits, full of charcoal pencils and sketch-pads. Mom enticed our next-door neighbors, Barbara and Nancy Fisher, to join her in producing charcoal still-lifes and outdoor scenes. Mom set up individual easels, trays for the pencils and pastel chalk, and served refreshments while the three of them worked. I don't remember anything Barbara or Nancy produced, but Mom's sketches of old barns, and tables of wine bottles, cheese, and fruit seemed perfectly rendered to my four-year old eyes.

I enjoyed standing near my mother in her basement studio as she drew, but she didn't get much enjoyment out of her youthful watcher.

"Don't look over my shoulder," she'd say, using an expression that I always equated with headaches. Maybe I was a headache back then, failing, as any child would, to understand that my mother both needed and wanted her space, her independence from the life above the basement. So for a short time, this basement space was entirely hers. I suppose that eventually, once-a-week art lessons became too infrequent to sustain any real momentum. When she abandoned the room, and my old toys, cards, and comics, took root there.

Mom was an orderly person. She saved all of my brother's and my landmark achievements in our baby books, and when I started school, she bought another School Days binder where she kept my report cards, Good Citizenship awards, even the love notes I received from my fifth grade girlfriend, Mary Jane. She saved what seemed to her to be momentous, important.

So perhaps the toilet overflowed, or perhaps, giving up her space made her bitter, and when the junk down there grew too unwieldy, she got rid of everything. Everything except my Dad's 78 RPM record collection, which gathered dust but sat on a closet shelf, just to the side of that toilet room. These survived the septic flood, I suppose, because they were kept above the fray. It's all so hard to figure, this room and what it meant to us.

Questioning the fate of my treasures and what happened in our finished, semi-secret basement room brings me back to the question of the room itself. Why was it built? For what purpose, or more importantly, for *whose* purpose?

"Storage," might have been the typical family answer, and yes, items were stored there, including years of Santa's presents before that season when my brother discovered our premature bikes. Yet that basement room existed long before either my brother or I was born, so what, if anything, necessitated being stored in this very strange, almost forgotten room?

§

Maybe you figured it out. Maybe I've known, too, for longer than I could admit. Or maybe it dawned on me only after I saw *The Help*. As a privileged white child growing up in the late 1950's and 60's, I had no reason to question the social mores of my community. Maybe I noticed more things than my peers did, and maybe my memory is better than theirs. And maybe I didn't want to solve the secret of this strangest room.

My mother's family employed maids long before I was born. The first was a woman named Mona Lee, who helped raise my mother. I don't know her last name; I met her only when I was seven or eight, when Mom hired her while our regular maid, Dissie Shepherd, was sick or on her one-week yearly vacation to see her family in Uniontown.

A third woman, Georgia Roberts, cared for my brother and me on certain Saturday nights when my parents went out to dinner and a movie, and my Nanny was off playing bridge with her cronies. Georgia had ten children, including a girl my age named Ellen Terry, after my Nanny.

I loved each of these women, though Dissie was my favorite, She'd play Concentration and Monopoly with me while she ironed. We'd watch "Lucy" and "Andy Griffith" and the afternoon soaps in those days before I started school. How can I tell you how much I loved Dissie, how much like a second mother she was to me? How hugging her felt like finding sanctuary?

After the house fire, and after we added those three new rooms, the space within my childhood world opened. Even though we now had two upstairs bathrooms, there were moments when both were occupied, not a pleasant alternative for a little boy in need. Instead of politely knocking, I'd go barging in to these spaces, often catching Mom or Nanny sitting still or trying to get up as fast as they could.

And sometimes I'd catch Dissie, too.

I wasn't trying to catch anybody. I just had to go, and even if one of those bathrooms were unoccupied, I had to get to the nearest one, because, as we all know, little boys usually hold their business past the safety time zone.

After the fire, Dissie used the upstairs bathroom—the older one in the hall off the breakfast room, but never the new one between my parents' bedroom and the den. I never knew, or thought to consider, whether this was a rule imposed by my parents, or if Dissie decided this herself. It's only now that I've considered the question.

Only now that, in the recesses of memory, I recall Georgia, and especially Mona Lee, descending those basement steps after our remodeling. Maybe I asked where they were going, and maybe they even said, "to my bathroom downstairs." Maybe I didn't ask but somehow knew. Life is full of such moments that both do and do not make a lot of sense.

I suppose that's the bathroom Dissie used, too, before the remodeling. How did things change? Who said what to whom? I saw Dissie emerging from the upstairs bathroom so often, that I either forgot, or didn't realize that this was anything outside of the norm. I'd love to ask someone what happened, how things changed, but everyone in this story except my younger brother Mike is gone now. And he doesn't know.

One more thing links this room and all that dwelled there once or used it. Like my comic books and baseball cards that I never saw again after leaving for school one sunny day, I never saw Mona Lee or Georgia after the last time they sat for me. I did see Dissie once after she left us.

I was married, and my wife and I saw her sitting on her front porch. We stopped, spoke for a while, and I hugged this woman I loved. She died a few years later, and though I felt it, I did nothing to mark the occasion of her passing. I stay in touch with her granddaughter now, all of this more than I did or can say about Georgia and Mona Lee who became castoffs from my world, or so it would seem from the way I unthinkingly let them go. To hear me talk, you'd think I loved my precious comic books more than them, these two women who ensured my safety. These three women who I always thought loved me.

§

Twenty-three years ago, my parents sold their house to an African-American family. The entire neighborhood, in fact, changed from being all white through the 1970's to virtually all black today. I have not set foot inside my old house since the weekend I helped my parents move some of their more precious items to the new house across town, which was also predominantly white back then, and predominantly black today. I helped my mother move some antique lamps and side tables that she didn't trust the movers to keep safe, and I helped my dad move his two power lawn mowers from that old basement room, out the third/side door, down the ramp, to his new garage. They completed their move the following week while I was back home in South Carolina with my wife and young daughters, living in a house with a completely finished basement, which does have a full bath that we added after moving in.

But I wonder about the family who moved into my parents' house. What did they think of the finished basement room, the door leading to nowhere? They'd never know about the floor damage, all the art and antiques, comics and cards that formerly slept there. Would they understand about the secret toilet and why it was there? Would they remark its existence at all? And if they did understand, would this knowledge cause them to wince, to remember, to realize that where they now lived was like so many other places back in those old days—an upstairs/downstairs world where rights and privileges had a scent and a meaning all their own?

A world from which, no matter how far you travel, you'll never be able to reconcile, or escape, certain secrets.

∫∫∫

# Thank You:

To Robert and Tim, for believing, reading, and publishing.

To the Bessemer Hall of History. May you last forever.

To The Bright Star, home of love and Snapper Throats.

To Kerry and Joni, for reading, writing, and inspiring.

To Max, my steadfast companion.

To Dissie, Mona Lee, and Georgia. Because you matter, and I felt your love. I hope I gave some back.

To my brother Mike, now more than ever.

To my wife and daughters, for reading (when I remind them), for loving, and for sharing a few secrets of their own.

# Acknowledgments

The essays in this collections were first published in the following journals:

Where Have We Been, Where Are We Going?  —*EMRYS* Journal

Daddy's Baby—*Lime Hawk* Journal

Loyalty Oath and Imagine There's No Underwear—*Cleaning Up Glitter*

Moose Park— *storySouth*

I Didn't Have That—*Coachella Review*

As I Lay Dreaming of S-Town—*Under the Sun*

Goin' Up the Country—*Eclectica* Magazine

Darkened Churches—*The Manifest-Station*

Secrets I'm Dying to Tell You—*Call Me [Brackets]*

# About the Author

Terry Barr, as one of his close friends has described him, is a "recovering Bessemerite." He thinks about his hometown likely more than he should, but that's because he has loved and been nurtured by so many people there. In his alternate life in Greenville, SC, he continues teaching at Presbyterian College, where, despite the disruption of spring semester 2020, he still enjoyed one of the best American Literature experiences with his students that he's ever had.

Barr and his wife, Nilly, do not get to see as much of their two daughters as they would like, but overall, they are both happy in knowing that all are safe and prosperous. As are the entire family's three dogs: Max, Warren, and Palmer.

Barr's essays can be found in journals such as *The New Southern Fugitives* and Greenville's *TOWN Magazine*. He writes almost daily on MEDIUM at medium.com/@terrybarr, so look for him there and at virtual parties near you.

Made in the USA
Columbia, SC
20 July 2020